The Spiral of Life

MONA ROLFE Ph D

The Spiral
of
Life

Cycles of
Reincarnation

SAFFRON WALDEN
THE C.W. DANIEL COMPANY LIMITED

First published in Great Britain in 1975 by
Neville Spearman Limited
Second Impression 1981

This new edition was published in 1992 by
The C.W. Daniel Company Limited
1 Church Path, Saffron Walden
Essex, CB10 1JP, England

© The C.W. Daniel Company Ltd 1975
ISBN 0 85435 432 8

Printed in England
by Hillman Printers Ltd
Frome, Somerset

Contents

Foreword

At this period in time, when there is a tendency to level humanity down to the lowest common denominator, many people are thirsting for an understanding of the reason we are engulfed by a flood of young souls who have neither the appreciation, nor the desire for a knowledge of spiritual values.

As we enter the Age of Aquarius there is an increasing need for an understanding of the power of the invisible rays from the higher planes which permeate our bodies and by virtue of which we live and move and have our being.

In these trance lectures Dr. Mona Rolfe gives the clue to the wisdom enshrined in the Book of Genesis; the creation of the soul and its journey on the spiral of life with responsibility for the evolution of the spark of life from its beginning in the mineral kingdom.

Born of Irish parentage, she was gifted with vision of the inner worlds from early childhood. She put aside these gifts to study medicine and psychology and to gain knowledge in many fields of research before developing her psychic-spiritual gifts to balance her intellectual achievement.

As we enter the new age her work is appreciated by a wider public and her inspired teaching combining the wisdom of the East and West gives a comprehensive philosophy of unique value.

B. Shephard

I. *Birth*

Birth is a wonderful miracle, which being one is yet three, which being three is yet one, the miracle which you know as birth, death and rebirth. They are all birth and yet we must distinguish these births, and as we distinguish them, come to a greater understanding of what they mean.

First we take the miracle of birth into the physical plane, and we look at it from two angles; from the angle of the children of the breath and from the angle of the life-spark. Briefly speaking, the great difference is this. The children of the breath are God-born, God-created, beings of light into whom the very breath of the Father-Mother God has been breathed; who belong to the light, who in their inner vision see the light and know God, even though in treading the path of matter they become soiled and smirched by the evil of the world.

But the children of the life-spark are children of the evolution. They evolve through the mineral kingdom, the vegetable kingdom, the animal kingdom into man. In that evolution they have within them that wonderful spark of light which is God's gift to this planet Earth, but they are not created of the Breath. They must achieve their soul through the pouring out of love to their fellow-men and to such fellow-men as can draw from God Himself His power of light and His love, and purifying themselves to become channels of the light, can pour out this life, this light, this power to all living things.

The Spiral of Life

The lump of coal, the diamond, the ruby, the amber which is washed up on the seashore, may seem to be inanimate things which have no life, yet within each one is that life-spark which is of God. When the life-spark begins to move through the soil, having passed the mineral kingdom to become the growth of the plant, it becomes a living thing which man can touch and see. When you tread upon the grass under your feet do you think of the life which is within it, or do you thank God that that life is being poured generously from that grass into your being for your strength and your upbuilding? You see the grass and it is a matter of course. You see the tree and you rejoice in the shade of it. Do you realise that these are living things to whom you owe thanks for all that they give you? Thank them mentally for all that they have done for you, then will they more graciously pour out their power upon you, for they draw their power from the life-spark, which is God in the form of earth, whereas man draws his God-force from God direct. Yet though the tree realises this gift from God, man rarely realises how the glory of God is within him from the spirit. The tree responds and gives us the power to draw upon the ethers of light and, through those ethers of life and light, to draw within itself the very spirit of God. Thus it grows and becomes beautiful and gives generously to mankind.

You move from the tree to a bed of flowers and you see their glory of colour, their light, and you realise how generously the life-spark is fulfilling its purpose, and all the time the same process is at work you thank God for the beauty of the flower.

The life-spark comes through the animal kingdom from the very lowest form of life to the highest; each according to its capacity has the power to draw upon the light, the life-spark, for its very existence, and where we touch animals which are brought into close contact with man we realise that there is some other force working there, for these are the product of the life-spark which was enabled to draw the ethers of light, the spirit of God, from the tree, or the blossom or the blade of grass. These have become creatures from the generosity of giving which man has shown, to return, either near or far from man, in their next life.

To those that have not evolved through this group, this method of evolution, there is nothing but death and decay, but to the animal there is a soul forming, for man has given back the love of God to the vegetable kingdom through that mass of light from which the soul is formed. When the animal that is wrapped in the love of man and draws very close to the life of man returns after death, he returns as a spark of the spirit of God and a portion of that great thing we call the group soul. According to the measure of love which man has given the animal, so the portion of the group soul is strong or weak, until there comes a time when it is strong enough to be detached from the group soul and to become incarnate in the body of primitive man. Go where you will among the primitive races of today, you will find some souls of great beauty, souls which through their group soul incarnations are brought very near to the heart of man and are warmed by the love of man which man radiates from God.

There are an enormous number of group soul children of the evolution, incarnate in the bodies of white men and women. Their whole evolution depends entirely on how the children of the light react towards them. Do you give them hatred and misunderstanding, or do you endeavour to see with their minds, to draw the power of God to open their eyes, and if you have such a child in your family, do you give it love or hatred, anger or compassion? Do you encourage it or do you shut it out?

We must come to an idea of the great responsibility which lies with the children of the breath moving through the evolution on earth, as to whether they give love and understanding, or hatred and cause despair. They are difficult, these children of the evolution. They do not face life as you do. They know nothing and certainly believe nothing of God, but they are here for you to teach, and you who are children of the breath must realise the difficulty of their path, even if they do not realise that difficulty themselves. They must achieve God, whereas you *know* Him, and when we use the word 'know', we are sending out a vibration on the ether of strength beyond your understanding, for only the children of the breath have the privilege of knowing God in all His glory, for they are created children of the breath.

In the beginning existed only the Holy Trinity, Father, Mother and Son, and it seemed good to our Father-Mother God that there should be more of that great beauty of the heavenly spheres spread out on the ethers of light. Therefore He came down in all the glory of the Trinity to a lower sphere and He created yet other Son-daughters, children of the rays of power and glory which are His children of the light.

Then Satanaku brought sin very close to the planes of light, and our Father-Mother God saw that it was good that yet more beings of light went forth, and He commanded His great Son-daughters whom He had created of His own Breath that they should bring forth children, children of light and glory in whom our Father-Mother God breathed the breath of life and called His own.

There came a time when these children of the light went out far and wide into the great Temple of Glory which lay below the God-sphere, and from that Temple of glory to a Temple which was known as the Temple of the Crown. It was built on a great height in a wonderful land which many of you call the Garden of Eden and was a wonderful land of light and glory. There they brought with them the glory of the God-sphere. They built a Temple, and in that Temple was ever light and glory, and round that Temple were great gardens where the evolution of the life-spark went forward continually through plants and trees and flowers, but not into any further creation, for the need for that had not yet arisen.

The child of the breath, created perfect Son-daughter of our Father-Mother God, may be a Son-daughter very close to Him by birth and descent, or he may be a Son-daughter far removed from Him by birth. Whichever he is there is ever that golden cord of light which binds him to his Father-Mother God, which gives him the knowledge, which gives him a sense of duty, which gives him an understanding of truth and light. The child of the breath who was born from light, who is called forth from light, who becomes a living, created being of the ether of light, a living soul, because our Father-Mother God has breathed into him the breath of life; who, adult, able to think and serve God and praise God and worship Him, and understanding that these great attributes of God, praise and worship, are not to be put into corners at the end of a day, but belong by right to God, is linked to God, and drawn close to God whenever He uses these attributes.

There came a moment when Satanaku did endeavour to create. He misused the word of power and endeavoured to breathe the breath of God into the creatures of his creation. These became crawling monstrosities, ugly to look at. Therefore, our Father-Mother God called together his children of the breath and He sent them out on a great mission to the children of darkness. From that mission they have gone forward, ever bringing the knowledge and the power of God with them into life.

The birth of a child of the breath is planned long long before he comes to earth. His parents are chosen frequently when they are only small children. Born under certain Zodiacal signs and the influence of certain planets, they will have the power to prepare the life which is just suited to this child's incarnation, and the soul of the child must study many, many years in your time in the Halls of Learning, the Halls of Endeavour and the Halls of Spiritual Enlightenment before he can come to earth and dwell in the physical body, part of God, a living soul, suffering the imprisonment and the limitations of the earth life.

When the time is dawning when he must draw near the earth, he is called for a special interview with the Master under whose guidance his life has been planned, and tests are applied to him to see whether he is really able to fulfil the life which has been chosen, and then he sets off.

If you could imagine a picture of the soul setting off on the path to birth you would see nothing but a flash of light, a ray emanating from the Father-Mother God, and within that ray a tiny globule, looking no bigger than the tip of your finger, leaving all the glory and peace and the beauty and the love of God, carrying that tiny

13

fragment of each to his earth life.

He will suffer birth and death in the ether in every plane through which he passes; his life in each plane depends upon the plan which has been made for him, and as he proceeds on his journey, he adopts at each birth a denser garment of ether until, when the moment for the birth of the infant arrives, he comes close to the mother, a being of light; and the mother feels him and knows the glory which is coming to her.

Here you have the explanation of the Annunciation of Mary; the moment when the Mother realises the glory which is coming, the moment when that ray of light from the very Breath of God touches the mother and gives her to know that all is well, and that this child which is coming to her is of the Breath and of the Glory of the Light.

During the coming of the child, the soul which shall soon be born stands many times besides the mother, watching and guiding the preparations for his life in the physical body, until all things are ready and, once more, just before birth into the physical body, he is permitted to return to the plane from which he comes, to make obeisance to his Master, and to say he is ready.

He has made this great journey from the planes of light with two other guiding spirits, spirits who have been chosen as the right ones to help him tread the difficult path, to help him and guide his footsteps nearer to God. He will have on the right side of him his doorkeeper, and on the left side his spiritual guide, who remains beside the mother during her hours of pain and watches with care the coming of the soul, waiting for the moment of the first breath; and who knows from the tone and the sound of that cry which comes on the first breath whether all is well or not.

By 'All is well' we do not always mean what you mean, for sometimes the most crippled body has the greatest light of God within it.

So comes the child of the breath into the birth of life. But ever the life-spark, the child of the evolution, must achieve a soul, and as the child of the breath comes down from glory into matter, so must the

14

child of the evolution raise himself from matter towards glory, until the moment comes when the breath of God is breathed within him as a reward for his efforts, and he returns, still a child of the evolution, but with the living soul of the breath.

2. *Death*

It is particularly in connection with those who live the intensely material life that we want to consider death. For death is a great reward for a life well spent – spent in God's service, in service to humanity, in teaching spiritual law and brotherly love, and in living according to the law of God from sunrise to sunset.

Death is a miracle; death which reveals the truth to man – not man as you see him, but man as God sees him, with his heart laid bare and open to the rays of glory.

You must remember that you are moving towards a new age, in which death will be unknown. We shall not think of people as 'dying' young or 'dying' old. We shall not think of death as tragedy. We shall realise that when the work which someone has been ordained to fulfil in service to God is completed, the time for the imprisonment in the physical body is at an end. For an imprisonment it is.

In the new age the spirit will predominate and man will just be taken to God when he has completed his work. There will be no dwelling on the lower astral planes. There will be no wandering in the darkness of the astral world, trying to pierce that darkness for some contact which will explain what has happened to the poor soul who wanders. There will be no lifting of the vibrations after mental suffering and mental testing to a plane higher than that lower astral. There will be no wandering about in the Garden of

17

Remembrance till you meet those who are looking for you from the other side of life. You will merely lay down your tools of office and, placing yourself in a receptive condition and relaxing the physical body, you will be taken directly by your guides and the messengers of God to the plane to which you belong. You will not be a stranger to that plane, because you will have entered it many times in sleep, as you do now, but with many differences, and you will leave behind you the radiance of your life. Because only when you have achieved and fulfilled the plan of your life will you be able to move onward and upward to a higher service.

There will be no sorrow. There will be nothing but joy, in the same way as you rejoice when your son is called to take up a position in another country which means pride of place and great monetary values to you today. That soul who loves you in the future will shed his radiance direct upon you, and you who are his mother, if it is your lot to remain on earth, will realise and know that in all ways you have fulfilled the law of God and trained your son to take his place in the world of light.

It is the same work that you are doing in this life. You are given charge of souls, either as a teacher in groups, or as an individual in the bond of marriage, or as a mother, or a father with the love of the child, or children, and we must remember that every action of those children reflects upon yourself. These children are lent to you by God; they come from God; they return to Him. To you is entrusted the training and the up-bringing of a living soul. Do you wish to draw the soul to the service of God and train the child through the eyes of the soul, or do you wish to draw out the personality and let that personality dominate the life of the little one?

When the moment comes for your son, or your daughter to go away from you, do you ask yourself if every step has been taken according to the law of God, or do you sit and weep for the loss of the physical child? Do you haunt the cemetery gates and through your sorrow add to the burden of those poor souls who haunt the astral plane and gather round these places of death and decay?

Or do you raise your head and say, 'It has pleased God to take my son; his work is finished'?

Let us not mar this picture by dwelling on the conditions of the astral plane, but rather let us realise the tremendous preparations which are made for the change you call death, and those preparations which are made on the other side of life.

Those who belong to spiritual-thinking groups and know much of the things of the spirit, know and realise the tremendous power of the soul for good or ill. Therefore the actions, the thoughts, the sentiments just before death are always either a strengthening force or a darkening force to the passing soul. Those who know and understand the unfoldment of the consciousness will not attempt at the moment of death to hold the spirit in the body. If you come to old age and feel very weary and know that you have become a misfit in the world of men, do you sit down and moan about it, or do you ask yourself what task for God have I failed to fulfil?

When the moment of death comes, whether it is for young or old, a call goes out from the plane to which the soul belongs. That call is symbolised by your orthodox church people as a trumpet, but in reality it is not that at all. It is a long drawn out bell-like note, the note of your archetype. It can be heard by your soul but not by your personality, and therefore, if your soul is developed spiritually it will command your personality and it will say to your personality, 'The call has come; our work together is finished', and those words will be accepted by the personality. It is that acceptance on the part of the personality that makes death swift and easy. It is the non-acceptance on the part of the personality that makes the end of life sad, miserable and long drawn-out. For the longer the space of time between the going out of that call and death itself, the fainter the memory of the sound of the call becomes, and the soul ever day by day loses its grip more and more, the personality gaining the dominance. The little faults of the personality, the dark thoughts, the quick temper, the jealous anger, the vindictiveness, the spite, the malice, all of which the soul has spent a number of years in trying to overcome, all come to the surface and the soul in sadness sees

19

itself hated and disliked by all who attend it and wait upon it. That is why death in old age is so often a calamity. But there are old people you visit who are sweet and gentle and kind, who have yet a little bit of work to finish which the soul must achieve before the passing. The personality will have slipped into the background, the soul, with its great strength and spiritual knowledge, will come forward and shine through the eyes, and it will at all times keep the personality just down here where it should be, and day by day it will grow stronger with the power of the spirit, because a soul of that type can absorb the power of spirit and live very near to God.

Once the call goes out, your place upon the plane to which you belong is prepared; it is like a little cubicle set aside for you; it is decked with the colours of your rays; it is beautified with the glory of your good works; it is harmonious and sweet and exquisite, as all souls are in the spirit.

We are above the astral plane now. It will have hangings of glory and light and yet it will be solid enough to form a protection; and because your knowledge of God and the things of the spirit will have taken all fear out of your material life, and because your needs have become very simple materially, when the times comes for you to go in old age, that place will be waiting for you. It will be kept swept and garnished, but only when the moment approaches for your passing, for the only thing which can achieve the final moment of death is the loosening of the bond of free-will which binds you to the earth.

There are many souls who will tell you they want to go, they are old, they are tired, they are weary, and earth holds them no more. They are usually people of very dominant nature who have no desire at all to approach the world of spirit, who find too much interest in the power of the personality and the exercise of their own free-will. Their paths may be weakness and suffering, their will still dominating their soul. The only thing which can release the soul is the submission of the will, and when once that is done, passing is so easy. The moment that the soul is loosed from its dominance, there is placed in that little cubicle a bowl of blossoms; those blossoms

20

are your own special flower of life; you will have met them in many lives and loved them and not known why. But the moment that the sleep of death is finished and the soul wakes in its new surroundings, the first thing that the eye lights upon is the blossom to which the soul belongs and which belongs to the soul.

But what a different picture we find. That is the miracle of death, for it is a miracle, and when you realise that for a long time before your death many messengers (sometimes in the case of a great soul, many angels) are preparing to descend from plane to plane and meet the soul and take it to its home, you will understand the tremendous beauty when the gates of death are open. If you can hold these pictures in your mind, never again will you sorrow.

There are some·souls for whom it is part of their path on earth and the earth life to spend a period of time in the astral plane, going and returning, and among these souls are many intellectual people and learned men. When they dwell in the astral plane in death it is usually because they have work to do on the astral plane in the same way as they had it to do upon the earth, which will prevent the call going out in all its fullness until that work is completed on the astral. Among these men you have many who have come back to teach men about the continuity of life and whose duty it is to prove as discarnate souls the existence of the personality, and it is part of their plan of life to do so.

How different is the passing of the man who knows not God; who has never had any spiritual leaning or desire; who has never touched this knowledge which you are touching; the man who lives purely for the personality. When the moment of death comes, the call goes out in exactly the same way, but it goes out from the seventh plane of the astral, and therefore his progress is slow. The passing of the soul will be slow, and the change between the etheric world surrounding the earth and the earth itself will be almost imperceptible. These have not prepared a place for themselves in the worlds of light. Therefore, just as they worked their way through earth conditions to complete security and monetary strength and power, they will have to work their way by the sheer

21

force of themselves through the astral worlds to the Garden of Remembrance, and when they reach the Garden of Remembrance they will be met by their friends. Those who pass to the plane to which they belong return to the Garden of Remembrance many times, but that is very different from having to earn the entrance to the Garden of Remembrance by a very difficult life in the astral plane. The darkness is very often quite dense round the earth plane. They flounder, they do not know what they are doing, and messengers go down from high planes to guide them and to strengthen them. All the same, just as they have earned their experience of life in the physical body on the earth plane, so must they have earned their experience of life in the astral body in the astral world.

You are here, not just to live through a span of years in the physical life, but you are here to strengthen and prepare your soul that it may be strong enough to leave the free-will out of the picture altogether when the times comes for you to pass into the glory and the gates of death.

You are here as teachers. To you we look to take the fear of death from all who touch it. You must learn to understand the hearts of your fellow men that you may give, when they sorrow after death, strength and courage and the right occupation to fill the gap, and through your contacts to strengthen the soul, that the soul may realise the glory of death and of life everlasting.

3. *Rebirth*

The question of rebirth seems to you children of the earth something intensely hard, and even at times cruel. It is not so at all. When you set your child out on the path of life, you choose for him the best school which your means will allow you to pay for and you choose for him a school which will educate him to the position in life which he will be called to fill. You know within your own heart more or less what type of life your son will take up, and whether he chooses business or a professional career, you know that he will mix with people of a certain taste and understanding. You lay the foundation for that life in the moment that you choose his school; and when you choose the school you are continuing your own training, for it is not possible to suppose that you would ever choose a school of a different way of life from your own, for you desire your child to hold to the moral and religious principles which you have taught him from babyhood.

Life is exactly the same for all of you. It is a school to which you return to learn, and God, placing you where you are, did so after all plans had been prepared by the Master who guides you, that you might take your place in life as a grown man in exactly the position which will help you to fulfil your path in life.

You are born under certain stars and planets. You may perhaps scoff at astrology, and if you only touch the astrology of the daily papers it is not surpising that you scoff at it, but the chart of your

23

life rightly drawn by a good astrologer can show you where you have failed in your past lives, what lessons you have to learn in this life, and what type of life you must come to in the world of spirit.

All men and women incarnate once every 200 years from the time that they achieve a soul through the life-spark, or the time that they are created children of the breath. There is a very great deal to do in the planes of spirit between one incarnation and another.

There is a feeling in some orthodox people that God calls all discarnate souls before Him and gives judgment upon them, but that is not the case. All souls in their two hundred-year cycles are responsible to God for their lives. That is true, but they do not come to God until they have taken their final testing, that final testing which is so important to prove whether the soul is really strong enough to meet God face to face.

Man is his own judge. That is why the exercises of retrospection are of such vital importance, because through those exercises you learn to see into your own heart and to know where you have done wrong and where you have done right. It does not do to go about the world criticising other people; it is much better to spend the time criticising yourself. Were you just in this? Were you right in that? And so on, until you find for yourself your own besetting sin.

If you have a chart of the heavens done at your birth, and every time you find a weakness in your own heart you refer to that chart of the heavens, you will be able to tell whether it is something purely of the personality or whether it is something karmic which must be cleared in this life; whether you have come to overcome a very dark and hard path or whether you have come back (still with a hard path) with a heavy load of karmic debts which you must pay.

Why is all this important? Because once you have left the physical behind, before you can dwell in the world of spirit, and that is the world that lies above the astral plane (men do not dwell in the astral plane; they abide there, but they do not dwell there — above the astral plane they dwell), you must have judged yourself, your actions on earth towards other people and your actions towards God. Then, once you have realised that and received it into your mind quite clearly, you will be taken by your guides, your doorkeeper and your spiritual guide, to the Master who rules your life, to be examined.

It is possible that this examination may be nothing more than just a blessing or a humbling of yourself and meeting with a great Being of light and a feeling of unfoldment in that light. But if within a certain period you have not judged yourself, then the meeting will be somewhat different. But from the moment that you have met your Master and he has laid his hand in blessing on your head, you are ready to plan your next incarnation. That next incarnation will be twofold in karmic condition, because you will probably have a certain amount of karma from the distant past which you have not entirely cleared and you will have karma which you have incurred in this very last life. Unless you have been strong enough to clear that karma step by step as you have gone forward in this life, that karma will be an added burden in your next life.

As soon as you have realised under those who guide you that the time has come for you to reincarnate, you will take yourself to the Lords of Karma and you will place before them the karmic conditions which you have failed to clear, the karmic conditions which you were not called upon to clear in that last life because it might have become too heavy, and the karmic conditions which you had created in the last life of all, and then they will decide the type of life which you must take: whether you must come back to handle wealth and power and understand it and use it wisely, or whether you must come back into a very humble position and learn humility and service.

From the moment that the Lords of Karma have given you permission to reincarnate at the end of your two hundred year cycle you will begin to make preparations. Those preparations will be made under the guidance of your doorkeeper, with your spiritual guide to bring the light from the higher planes of spirit to you, and from time to time, the pointing finger of your Master to show you the way. These preparations will take a long time, and when they are completed and the soul sets forth on its journey towards the earth again, that soul may belong to a plane quite a long way from the astral plane and therefore the progress into the world of earth will be slow. He must suffer birth and death in every plane he touches. In the etheric planes it is not the shedding of a body but the adoption of a body that counts, and therefore, as the soul descends, he adopts a denser etheric covering with each plane of life, until the moment comes for him to stand and wait for his birth upon the earth.

From the time that a soul has received permission from the Lords of Karma to reincarnate, no other service is demanded of him, and all the millions of debts which are asked of the disembodied soul in the world of spirit pass him by. He is set aside. He is a soul on his way to earth, and though he meets in his progress hundreds of souls whom he has already met and hundreds of others whom he has to meet, they do not touch or deter him at all from the path of reincarnation.

When he reaches the seventh plane of the astral he finds himself once more in the Garden of Remembrance. It is here that he must remember his life in the world of spirit and he must remember his last life on the earth, that he may model himself anew for the coming life. And in these Gardens of Remembrance it is the duty of many who help him, to bring towards him people (souls who are also discarnate) whom he must meet upon the earth plane.

This, although it sounds very unimportant, is one of the most important periods of the reincarnating soul, because if he comes to earth and blots out the whole of his memory he will find that nobody makes the least difference to him. Whereas if he comes to earth with the full knowledge of the meetings and the acquaintances and the friends he has met in the Garden of Remembrance, he will have a very much clearer idea of the work which lies before him. The finest foundation for the life in the world of man is a long period in the Garden of Remembrance. Why do you so often turn with dislike from the most charming people? Why are you drawn to men and women whom your friends will not look at or attempt

26

to understand? Go back in your memory to the Garden of Remembrance and you will realise what an important part they played in that particular portion of your life there, because they had come into your earth life at the moment that you met them in the Garden of Remembrance, and they had brought with them things from the past which it is of vital importance that you should understand.

When you dislike someone, do not think it is always that you must avoid them. In the majority of cases that dislike is due to the fact that you know you have a very unpleasant duty to repay to them, or that there is some experience which you must share with them which you dislike and desire to avoid.

When the two hundred years of incarnation is completed and the number of incarnations is also completed a very important time waits for the incoming or home-coming soul.

You do not have that joy in departure, until the moment has come for you to complete your great testing time, and that testing time in most cases will be very severe if you are to hold any place at all near to God. It will cut you off from lives in which you have known ease and comfort. It will place you in a very humble position. It will place you where you will all the time take orders from people who know very much less than yourself. It will be only in your own moments of silence that you will be able to withdraw into the silence and make contact with God, and know and realise that the moment for your release from the physical body is not yet; that there is still something which you must complete before you cross the bridge of death. It is only when you have completed that testing time that you will be permitted to see God, and then you will be, from the moment of death, conducted swiftly through the astral to the plane to which you belong, and swiftly before the Lords of Karma, to give them an account of yourself in the world of men.

The Lords of Karma will place upon your brow the jewel which represents the overcoming of all things. The Lords of Karma are unfailing in their justice; they will not accept a soul that has not completed his own self-examination and self-judgment; they will

27

only accept a soul who has completed his path on the earth with understanding and with courage. When you leave the hall of the Lords of Karma you will move, even in the world of spirit, as you have never moved or known yourself to move before. It is a movement of swiftness, of complete sureness, of lightness ineffable, and of glory, for with the placing of that jewel on that brow, the Lords of Karma have placed upon you the seal of release from incarnation into the physical body again.

You will return to the place where your Master dwells, and you will remain awhile with him that he may partake of the strength and light which have been given to you in the ornament of the jewel, and then together you will make your preparations of humility and purification and travel to the Presence of God.

It is possible that when you reach our Father-Mother God you will not see Him. The light, even with your light, will be too strong, but you will hear His Voice – a Voice as of many waters, a Voice which holds all the wisdom of earth and heaven combined. The words which He speaks to you will be spoken to you only because you wear His jewel in your brow, and they will be spoken upon your own archetypal note, so that none in all that great company of angels and saints can understand what God says to you.

You will go for a period of rest and refreshment, and you will forget the weariness of earth life. You will forget the cold stones of the church in which you worshipped those early winter mornings; you will forget the hard labour which was demanded of you, and you will draw for a while very near to your Master, for until then your Master has been a Being of light, distant from you, but from that moment you and he are Elder Brothers for all time, and you dwell as brothers and you rest as brothers, and you drink deep of the Peace of God which passeth understanding.

You will go where God commands you, until the moment comes when God will call for volunteers for some great work on earth. Then you will find that, though you have made up your mind that nothing will ever induce you to return to the earth again, yet when God speaks to you on your own archetypal note, as He speaks to thousands in the same words in the vibration which each individual hears differently, you will know that you are God's servant for all time, and that if He has need of you, your duty lies at His side.

Whether God speaks to one or whether He speaks to millions, each soul can only hear His Voice on his own archetypal note, and if the soul does not go out to meet God the archetypal note falls on deaf ears.

4. *Karma*

There is nothing in the working of God's law for man which is so misinterpreted and misunderstood as Karma. Karma in plain English is the law of cause and effect and the working out of that law. It is much simpler to say 'Karma' than to use those two long sentences and so we use the Eastern word 'Karma', which really only means the working out of God's law.

When you speak of Karma you are speaking of the working out of the law; therefore you do not say 'the working out of Karma'. Karma is the complete working out of God's law for man.

Karma exists upon the physical plane. When man, the soul, is imprisoned in the body of flesh, he is working out the law of cause and effect. But Karma does not end with the death of the body; a certain amount of Karma is worked out upon the astral plane, even in the seventh plane of the astral plane, and that is a very important place for those who are subject to Karma to meet. Karma does not continue once you have left the astral plane.

No soul who has progressed beyond the Garden of Remembrance, that is, the seventh plane of the astral plane, can at any time be subject to the law of cause and effect, but all souls can be subject to the law of cause and effect in the astral plane; and in the physical plane it is the most important thing which reincarnated man can touch.

There are souls who are on earth at the moment in very large numbers to complete their last testing. These are souls who have completed their correct number of incarnations on the physical plane, who have come into incarnation as a matter of routine every two hundred years, roughly, (with exceptions of course), and who are now ready to take up their special spiritual work for God. Before they can come to God and present themselves before Him, before they are strong enough to touch His glory and His power, even from the outermost fringe of the plane where He dwells, they must return to earth for one more vital and important incarnation and that incarnation is entirely free from Karma, because if they had brought into the world of spirit any karmic debts from their sojourn in the physical body on earth, they would not have been cleansed and purified sufficiently to take this last testing.

Therefore you are moving today in a very unusual material-spiritual world. You are touching more closely than you have ever done before the children of the life-spark, who in their journey through evolution are preparing themselves to become the children of God; you are touching many great and small souls who are here to clear the most extraordinary karmic debts; and you are touching hundreds of thousands of great souls who have completed their periods of incarnation and have returned to earth completely free from karma.

These last souls are perhaps to you impersonal, if you are not one of them. They have a high sense of duty and loyalty, and they are to be found, as a rule, among the very humblest of your citizens, for humility is one of the great virtues which admits them to God.

Therefore, there are children of the light who are on earth to-day and bear no karmic burdens; there are children of the evolution who, because they have not evolved to the conditions where they can own the law of God as God's children, are also without karma, and in the centre of all these you have great and mighty souls and some small children of the breath of God who are bearing their karmic burdens in a world of darkness and despair.

We cannot say which is carrying the heaviest burden or the most difficult life. It is the fact that when these four categories are mingling together as one nation, one religion, one band of politicians that the difficulties occur. There are hundreds of people whom you meet in your daily life who do not understand the language you speak. You both speak the English tongue; you were perhaps born within a stone's throw of each other, and yet with heart and head you fail to speak the same language.

What brings into operation karmic law – the law of cause and effect? One thing only, the free-will of man. The child of the great testing is without free-will, for through many lives he has so learnt to submit himself to the will of God that he sees God's finger pointing the way; within him is that great faith which tells him that God will never forsake him and that though he is glad to go through suffering and tribulation, unhappiness, disease and sorrow, it is a testing time only. There will be no result on his fellow-man of any of his sorrow or disease or suffering; but he cannot pass disease from father to son as those can who bear the burden of Karma. He moves through the world entirely without free-will, guided by the will of God, living his material life without looking backward very much, and most certainly without looking forward very much. He knows that the tests which are applied to him are of his choosing, and that he has returned to earth to be tested and tried to the uttermost point of his physical and spiritual might, in order that he may never return to earth again, unless there is some special service for God which God will call him to fulfil, but which he will have the right to refuse.

The children of the life-spark are clear from the law of Karma. They have no free-will; they are children of instinct only; their only motive force is instinct. That is why they think of themselves only and forget their fellow-men, as the cat that desires to devour a small bird does not think of the feelings of the bird or the unhappiness of his master if he catches it; he wants the bird. He is guided by his own inner instinct which says 'That bird shall be mine'. So is the man of the life-spark a creature of instinct, and the instinct which is most strongly developed within him is self-love and self-preservation. He

33

does not care how many people are trampled under the hooves of the runaway horse so long as he escapes. He does not care how many lame or tired people are left behind when the omnibus moves forward too laden to carry any more, so long as he has pushed his way to the front and got his own place therein.

Between these two groups you have the mighty mass of souls who are endeavouring with understanding to clear karmic conditions and those who have no understanding and are moving blindly forward, buffeted from right and left, never fitting anywhere.

Of the former, those who understand the law of cause and effect, there is one very great and important thing to remember. From the moment that you begin to desire the awakening of the spirit and desire to study the law of God, there are those guided towards you from the world of spirit, who will weave round you a cloak of protection. They will use the ray on which you function, the ray to which you belong, and to that ray they will add other rays until you are enveloped on all etheric planes with a light and glorious canopy of ether. You can walk alone and draw that canopy towards you from the moment that you submit your will to the will of God, but if you set your own will at variance to God's will, if you forget that you have as great a duty to your neighbour as to God, if you forget that all men incarnate are God's children and that you have a duty to every individual one of them as they have a duty to you, you will walk through life just outside this etheric canopy and your whole life will be at variance with God. But from the moment that you begin to understand the working of God's law, and you realise your material responsibilities towards your fellowman, and your spiritual duties and responsibilities to God, from the moment that you hold our your hands and ask for power to be poured into you and cleanse and purify your soul that it may accept the glory of the spirit of God, then you are moving gently and slowly within this canopy, and there will be no more variance; things will fall into place. The etheric canopy will not prevent you from suffering, it will not make you fail in the repayment of your karmic debts, but it will strengthen you with the power of the spirit, so that no matter what befalls you, what anxiety, what disharmony, what physical fatigue and overstrain come to you, you cannot know fatigue, because you are under the protection of God as an individual soul, and you are treading the path in harmony with your plan of life, so that those who must approach you and link with you in your journey on the earth, can do so with perfect security, and joy will shine from your eyes.

So the law of karma comes into operation from the free-will of man. The free-will of man works upon the earth plane. It works after death upon the astral plane, until the soul has repaid every injury it has done to those who remain in the physical worlds. It is much easier to complete your karma in the physical body than it is to try and return from the astral plane and complete your karmic debts there, although from time to time some of the finest guidance comes to the students of the higher teaching from those who are expunging their karma by guiding him from the other side of life.

When the soul plans to come to earth he realises the karma he will have to carry, but he does not touch the memory, or understanding of that karma as he comes down through the planes of light and glory until he reaches the Garden of Remembrance. There, all is made plain to him with regard to karmic debts and karmic laws, and with regard to his own personal debts towards his fellows.

Karma, as you know from any text book, can be taken through many phases. A soul can return to clear karmic debts of a personal nature only; he can return to clear karmic debts of a community (a 'community' such as the Huguenots or any of the very early religious bodies); he can come to earth to clear the karmic debts of a king in whose service he failed in obedience to the laws of God. More important than all, he can come to earth to clear the karma of a temple which in the past has sinned grievously and deeply against the law of God, and to clear that karma because of his position as priest or high-priest or some other capacity in that temple of the past where darkness reigned.

There are some who, connected with the blood sacrifices of Atlantis, are still returning even today in an endeavour to clear those appalling conditions, and many of the cases of cancer which are untouchable and incurable are linked with the blood sacrifices of Atlantis.

There is racial karma and national karma, but the karma of the individual is the one that we should think most deeply about. Those who find that if today you err towards your fellow-man and that mistake hits you back, know and realise that you are one of those who have to return at the end of this troubled life completely clear of karmic debts.

5. *The Creation of the Soul*

When God creates a soul, He projects into the ether the power of His own spirit and that power of spirit moves through the ethers of light directed by the Will of God towards the earth. It is motivated by radiation and therefore contains all the seven rays of light and colour, which are also attributes of God. Having made contact with the lower ethers, this power of spirit – again by the Will of God – is divided and sub-divided into portions which are given life.

For quite a long period of time, a drop of spirit moves about in the fire fog of the middle ethers. When life comes to it, not yet the Breath of God, it is still spirit but it is no longer spirit in a mass but spirit divided into an individual self-creating unit, which grows and absorbs light and colour. As soon as the growth is ready for infusion, it is returned to God for the manifestation of spirit in such a way that it can become a living soul.

It is at this moment that our Father-Mother God breathes into this individual cell the breath of His very own life. That breath is the spirit essence which animates the soul, and the cell goes forth on its journey, growing, enlarging, absorbing light and darkness, or rejecting light and darkness. By the time it reaches the seventh plane of the astral, which you know as the Garden of Remembrance, it is a vital living created soul, part of God. It is in the Garden of Remembrance in those great temples of healing, those hospitals which lie behind the Garden itself, that the soul grows and develops.

37

It is here, in one of the schools of learning, that the mind becomes animated and within the soul begins its life function.

But all this time the soul is drawing sustenance from God alone, in the form of light and colour, power and love. It moves in the ether, mingling with souls who are recently discarnate and those who have been directed to the Garden of Remembrance to meet other souls about to return. From each it absorbs a little, in some cases the light of heaven, in other cases the light or the darkness of earth. It begins, as the mind grows, to be conscious of the thought force of those who wait in the Garden of Remembrance at the moment of death of those they love, so that they may meet and move with them in the Garden as soon as the cord is loosed from the physical body.

The important point of this period of development is the fact that all who meet in the Garden of Remembrance have already learned how to give, and it is their giving to each individual soul which gives that soul growth and life. Then there comes a moment when that soul is recalled to God for further preparation and it remains for quite a long period under instruction and under the guidance of those who know for what purpose this soul is being prepared. Then the moment comes when the soul is directed by God into incarnation. The soul under guidance must choose its own parents, and strangely enough the new soul frequently chooses parents who have wealth and power, and it comes to earth through the normal process of birth and death in every plane through which it passes on its journey.

Although the soul in the beginning may choose its parents it is not allowed to choose the sign under which it is to be born, and those first signs are chosen entirely according to the work that the soul has to do. If he has to come to earth as a warrior, he will be born under the sign of the warrior and under the planet that influences that sign. If it is the soul of a dominant woman, then it will be born in such a way that the dominance of that woman may be given leadership and understanding of leadership. But when coming into incarnation for the first time, the parents are always simple homely people. They may have wealth and power or they

38

may have an origin of peasant birth behind them – but they will most certainly give that one quality which is essential for the early growth of the soul, the power of love.

The personality is the cloak of the soul, for none, not even the parents are allowed to see the complete soul of the child. Only God sees that soul and knows it, but the personality is the mask or covering of the soul and that is chosen and prepared in such a way that the soul will be able to fulfil a period of life on earth which will concern its early development only. For the great point to remember in the newly incarnated soul, is that the portion of the spirit, the Light of God, which it holds is extraordinarily small and only by the right development of the personality can that soul hope to recreate the power of the spirit within itself, in order to return to God with the gift that God has given it doubled, amplified, more beautiful. You have an example of this, and a very good example, in the parable related in the New Testament of the Talents.

We now look at the incarnated soul many incarnations hence. It has returned to earth many times, learning under different masks, or personalities, the lessons which it has come to learn, and it is 'strapped' to the Wheel of Rebirth. It has now no voice in its incarnational problem except in the choosing of its parents. Those parents that are put before it are usually prepared by the Lords of Karma, and therefore are ready to accept the child when he indicates his preference for one particular couple. But the signs of the Zodiac which govern the personality change with every incarnation until the moment comes when the cycle of all 12 signs is completed, and the soul must now return to earth to accept the influence of the moon and the sun, but particularly the moon.

In accepting the influence of the moon there is the first merging between soul and personality, and it is at this moment that the soul may begin to guide the personality to raise its consciousness to the level of its own soul. No longer is the personality apparently without aim or object other than to develop the traits masked by those particular zodiacal signs. It now has a great purpose, the raising of the consciousness to meet the soul created by God, which

39

harbours and holds the Holy Spirit of the Father-Mother God Himself.

It is at this moment that life for the soul/personality becomes more difficult. For the personality must learn to know its own soul, to realise the purpose of its incarnation and to understand how, little by little and day by day, the whole of its life is turned over to God, for God to use it under His laws as He wills. The personality must pull itself together, it must become braced and strong. In the raising of its consciousness, it must be conscious of the act of the raising of the consciousness and conscious, too, of the presence of the soul.

During the early incarnations of these now advanced souls, we see many who have to return quite quickly in one incarnation after another under the same signs, in order to unfold and develop the personality, that it may raise itself and merge with the soul. That is why in life you meet some people who seem to have a natural and greater understanding of the handling of their own Zodiacal signs in such a way that they can, if they wish, fit into the meaning of those signs and guide their lives in accordance with their ruling. Because once you have had an incarnation under a given rising sign and a given sun sign, unless you fail in the moon period you will not find it difficult to remember the mistakes of the previous life which prevented you from attaining your soul.

The Third Initiation, the Temple of Ra-Amen, is the initiation known as the White Swan. All over the world today, hundreds and thousands of souls are undertaking the initiation of the White Swan, in which the personality must raise its consciousness until it becomes one with the soul. By this time personality and soul will have come to recognise the love and the power of God, to recognise also the purpose of their own life. In the determination that the soul shall predominate these people seek light, mental illumination, strength and purpose.

In this particular initiation the purification of the body is one of the most important links with all students, so that no darkness shall be held within the body which could prevent the entry and

40

manifestation of the soul, so that no darkness could be held in the etheric bodies which could prevent the personality from being raised to the level of the soul.

Those who gather in Sanctuaries today are working for just that note of progress and preferment through their esoteric studies and their work as healers, and through the work in the building of the foundation of their own Temple; the Temple in which they can come together and worship and study, and also the Temple of their own physical body which shall house the glory of the soul. You will remember the power and the importance of the full moon on this merging of soul and personality. It is a well known astronomical fact — not an astrological one, an astronomical one — that the Harvest Moon has the peculiar property of being able, on each of three successive nights of fullness, to rise and set at identically the same spot in the heavens. All other moons, except one moon in Spring, move slightly across the sky; they are not stationary, in a sense, as this one is. They rise and set at different points on each of the three nights of their fullness. But the moon of Spring, which is a new moon and not a full moon, has that property also, and that is because the radiations of light from the Father-Mother God towards his children are held strong and solid on those two important occasions.

You will find that the psychic power flows much more freely during the time of the Harvest Moon and of that new moon in Spring. You will find your soul hardly needs to call the personality into the silence of meditation, so ready is the personality to raise itself to the higher consciousness of spirit.

6.   *Three Stages of Reincarnation*

We are going to consider the meaning of the Labours of Hercules in the life of man and the symbolism attached to them.

The Twelve Labours represent the twelve middle incarnations of man. When we consider reincarnation we must divide the incarnations of man into three distinct groups, each group consisting of a number of incarnations, the number depending upon the karmic conditions and so forth that man must work out for himself.

The first group of incarnations consists of that period when man is creating his personality, when the soul created by God is commanded to journey to the Earth and to become incarnate in the body of flesh and grow up from childhood to manhood learning certain experiences of the personality alone.

By means of the journey down through the spheres the soul of man is projected and by the time that the soul reaches a point of incarnation for the first, second or third time — whichever it is – he is frequently entirely unconscious of the purpose of the journey he is undertaking, and therefore at the time of birth there is no personality created into which the soul can move and function. Often the soul departs from created man to stand beside him through life. This is the period of the incarnation of the new or young soul.

43

The Spiral of Life

When man incarnates under these conditions he usually lives a life of poverty and great physical difficulty, because it is only by the acceptance of the physical difficulty of life that man is able to appreciate the value of the soul and to express his desire for the soul to accompany him on life's journey.

He will probably be an extremely ignorant person, without desire for higher things, living from day to day. Imagine a lad of about eighteen, ragged and unkempt, emerging from a cellar where he sleeps upon straw, eating refuse and scraps thrown away by those who have more than he has. Here you have the picture of the soul in the first period of incarnation. If the soul is able to create a worthwhile personality during that period, we shall find a consciousness of soul developing in the personality and when the moment of death comes the soul will cross the Bridge, the body discarded. That would probably be a soul/body which had known no such thing as love during that period of existence, and after death the soul journeys back the way it has come to the place of waiting. At that moment the soul reaches the point where, having completed his first incarnation, he must learn, in the place where he finds himself through his development, certain lessons in order to be able to return to Earth and create a new body with the help of his parents in two hundred years time.

In that period of incarnation, the period of time between incarnations never varies; time is the important factor of life, for the soul must learn to complete his lessons in time to be ready. Otherwise, if the two hundred year period is completed, he must return incomplete to the world of men, and this makes life very difficult, because it means that he would not be ready, or able to meet those who will help him on the next stage of his earthly journey.

In the first incarnation he will make practically no friends; he will be a lonely person, because the only condition that is imposed upon him is that he shall create a personality suitable for the soul to control. If he is close in thought to his soul, the soul will be able to guide him, but if he is not close to his soul then he will have to tread the path alone, with very little understanding of material or spiritual matters.

So he spends another span of life on Earth. During this period, when we reincarnate once every two hundred years, we do not pass over very easily as infants. If we cross the Bridge of Death while still children or young people, if we are in such a mental condition at the age of roughly two or three that we are unable to conform to the pattern of physical life which is set before us, then we are called upon frequently to return and work out on the astral plane the conditions which have held us back during that incarnation. That is, when we reincarnate from the astral plane without waiting for the two hundred years to be completed. Such an incarnation is extremely difficult, because we depend upon returning to the place where we are called upon to learn and study, not in the Place of Light, but near the Place of Light. If we return very early in childhood, or youth we must return to Earth having passed the period of time in one or more of the astral planes, but without having any education for the next incarnation.

From this comes the theory which is often held that when a child passes over in infancy it returns very soon to the same parents to fulfil its life again. This does actually happen under certain conditions, occasionally. The soul that has only made part of the journey towards the Light after death will come back a very different person from the person he was before he took that journey in infancy or childhood.

The second period in reincarnation is of vital importance, because there is no compulsion at all about it. When we have completed the work we are called upon to do in the physical body and have cleansed and purified our souls from any karma which has been incurred in the two hundred year period of return, we are taken to a special planet, as souls of course, without the body. We learn and study the meaning of those previous incarnations, the meaning of the message that we carry to Earth, the meaning of the linking of the mind with the brain and the preparation of the soul for the work of God.

When we have mastered these lessons, and they are not easy to master, we are allowed to ask permission to reincarnate if we want to. But the desire to reincarnate does not come to every soul. There are many, many souls who do not want to reincarnate and who are never forced to do it, but the soul must reach a high degree of spiritual supremacy in order to reincarnate voluntarily and of his own free will.

That period of time is a long preparation, for in the Place of Light man must continually be called to service by the Father-Mother God and he must have learned to obey that call and to know and realise the purpose of his service in the Place of Light. Then when he starts his journey to the Earth he is permitted to choose his parents. The choice of parents is planned under very important guidance so that the advent of the child in the family shall assist the parents to fulfil their incarnations in service to God, and shall assist the child to work out his soul's salvation and to cleanse and purify any karma at all which has still to be cleared.

These plans for incarnation are not made or taken easily, for many souls come into the picture, or reach incarnated life to meet other souls. The soul must meet many hundreds of people in the physical body whom he has known in different guise in previous incarnations. Where he has given hurt, or harm he must be prepared to correct that harm even to giving himself suffering in the repayment of the debt. Where he has been helped he must be prepared to walk beside the souls that have helped him, in order that they together may fulfil a great task for God which can never be asked of the soul or fulfilled in the physical during the periods of compulsory reincarnation.

This is a very difficult period and it is a period when the soul must hold great strength of purpose. He must first of all have learned to obey the will of God and to accept His will only as guidance. He must learn to look at his fellowmen, deep into their hearts, and realise the spark of God-light, where it is placed and his work Has he to encourage it with friendship? Has he to r to educate the soul holding it, in such a way that he may fulfil all that he has come to fulfil?

Then there is another period, when having completed many voluntary incarnations the soul takes a long rest in the Place of Light and returns close to the Earth, under the guidance of God, to guide an individual soul of man. He will have had to learn the truth and the understanding of many lessons, some of which he may himself have failed, for through his failure he will be able to guide the soul he is called upon to strengthen and prepare. He will on some occasions be called to draw very near to souls in very humble conditions, but always the thing that stands out when he is called upon to guide a soul is the fact that from his own lessons, and the results of those lessons upon his soul and upon his progress in the Place of Light, he must draw the right examples for the guidance of the physical man or woman he is called upon to stand beside.

He does not make mistakes – he would not be there if he had not conquered the period of making mistakes – and he must learn, also, to stand aside when certain conditions must be borne entirely alone by the man he is trying to guide. There are many things which the guide or the Master you know in the spirit may never prevent you from doing, or oblige you to do. He merely places the proposition in front of you and then he knows and understands whether his teaching with you has been right, because it is your action, your thought, your reflection, which shows him whether his lessons have been rightly absorbed and you have been prepared for your task.

Then there is the third period when man who has learned all the experiences he is allowed to learn of life, is called upon by God directly to incarnate in a physical body for some special work or preparation, such as all those who are called upon today to hold the sharp steel, the cleansing instrument of steel, and press it through the heart of man in order to cleanse that heart for the coming of the New Christ.

So we return in thought to the Twelve Labours of Hercules. For Hercules represents physical man at his finest and strongest physically, a being absolutely able to face alone the conditions of physical life, holding the physical attributes which he needs for the fulfilment of those twelve great tasks. For these tasks are each symbolic of one compulsory incarnation, and no incarnated man or woman is allowed to escape them. He must pass through each one of those twelve tasks, physically strong, able to face whatever difficulties come to him in the physical plane, and yet unconscious of the God who guides him, unconscious of the glory of the Light from which he derives his power, unable to give thanks because he has no idea to whom he should give thanks, but determined to conquer.

Therefore those first incarnations of two hundred years may have to be taken two, three, or even four times each. That is why you find it so difficult to look upon the life you remember in the physical today and ask yourself: 'In which of those labours did I fail? In which of those labours did I fulfil myself? Which of those labours represents the greatest development for my soul?'

And as your soul progresses to voluntary incarnation you are given the memory of your success in the twelve labours of life, and that memory it is which guides you towards the spiritual strength of the Father-Mother God, which opens your eyes to the glory of God, which strengthens your soul with the love of God and which teaches you, because you have learned in a hard school, the work you have come to do in the name of God in the service of mankind.

7. Major Cycles of Reincarnation.

We know that the soul reincarnates into the physical plane, inhabiting a physical body, once in two hundred years, and that after a long period of these two hundred year incarnations the soul achieves mastery of itself and is given permission to stand back from compulsory incarnation.

That is the basis of the doctrine of reincarnation. The soul which is moving on the two hundred year spiral spends periods of between fifty and ninety years incarnate on earth in between each two hundred years, so that we find the soul incarnate in the flesh for a period of physical life lasting between fifty and ninety years, returning to the world of spirit to dwell in the world of spirit for two hundred years before he incarnates again.

Those two hundred years are not just spent in waiting. A large portion of the beginning part of that span is spent in clearing up the muddles and the confusions which the soul has created around himself in the body. Then there is a long period of teaching, which we, perhaps, in the world of spirit would describe as general teaching – learning to improve our way of worship, learning to accept a greater humility, learning the glory and the beauty of forgiveness and learning also the tremendous value of the Grace of God. So that with this teaching in between incarnational periods we find the soul gentler, more God-like when he steps out into the moment of preparation for his return.

49

The Spiral of Life

Above all, our beloved Father demands that the soul shall have overcome, that it shall have a clear vision of God and a knowledge of the purpose of God and life, and on that foundation our Father will build His advice for the next incarnational period.

The incarnational period will be undertaken to clear the karmic debts of the soul created in previous lives. He will be called upon to make certain contacts in the physical body among those whom he has loved and helped and hurt and perhaps hated. These contacts will be very well and truly considered and prepared so that the soul may take step by step the points which he must touch. Where he has helped and loved, those souls in incarnation will be called upon to give him help and love in this next life. Where he has hurt and hated he must suffer himself from the power of the hurt which he has given, till he is able to hold out his hand to the soul he has wronged and make friends.

Therefore, the purpose of the soul in reincarnation is to cleanse and purify himself from the karmic debts of the past and with the love and gratitude of his friends to build a sure foundation for the Temple of the future, so that he will be given the power for the manifestation of God's law and he will be withdrawing darkness by wiping out his own evil deeds.

This is not done haphazardly. During the period that the soul has been in the world of spirit he will be shown every move, every point in connection with his life and he will of his own volition offer and learn how to put right those matters which must be adjusted.

In addition to these two types of souls, those he has loved and those he has disliked, he must make contact with a large number of other souls who will appear to him insignificant and are very often substitutes for people he must meet in that final incarnation when all come together. The place of the substitute is not an easy one because it means that some soul has withdrawn or fallen out who should be playing a major part in the picture of that man's life. If he falls out, another must take his place, and he then becomes a substitute. The positive karmic light which will be given to such a substitute is a very great reward and therefore every soul preparing to come to earth must know that on his right hand are souls he has loved in his last incarnation and helped, and on his left hand the souls he has hurt and disliked, and behind them a number of people, souls who are called to play a part during that man's life who are not actually the souls he met before but substitutes. The substitute can be arranged from the beginning, so that he comes to earth definitely in the plan of life for man, or he can be arranged to be ready to slip in at any time when an important contact falls out.

In that last moment, when all the two hundred year periods are completed, the soul after death at the end of that period is received into a place of light, where those whom he has helped to complete their own karmic debts will come and do him homage and say farewell to him, before he goes into those great Halls of Learning. There he is now free to roam, until, from within his own heart he is moved to ask that he may reincarnate again.

At the end of every five hundred years there comes into operation an even vaster scheme of reincarnation, because at the end of one of these periods of five hundred years which depend upon the Moon's phases and the opportunities the Moon gives to man to complete his work for God, whole periods will reincarnate together. You will find that a whole Atlantean period will reincarnate together, both from the Temple on the Heights and from the children of the Valley. You will find that a whole period of history such as the Tudor period, the Stuart period, the Georgian period, and the time of the French Revolution is of course particularly important, will bring into incarnation many thousands of souls into one broad spot and those groups of souls come back with a group spirit (not the group soul, but the spirit of the group developed to a very large extent), so that they do definitely cling together, hang together, hold together, because they know that they cannot fulfil the purpose of their incarnation unless they do hold together.

The number of souls incarnating on the two hundred-year cycle at such periods is very small indeed and they will be completely absorbed by the five-hundred cycle, which are called Temple

51

cycles, for they are all either concerned with the Temple of God or the temple of man which is the court. Therefore, the Temple of the Spirit, the Temple of God, will be represented by one group and the Temple of the court will be represented by another.

There are also the enormous numbers of men and women who incarnated down the ages into monastic life and these will return in the same numbers as they were incarnated in the monastery and the convent but into ordinary material life. They will very soon be drawn aside from the crowd of men and you will find these always where there is a gathering from great distances round one Temple or one Sun, for they are spread over widely different areas to fulfil their own physical life and clear their own karma, but also to live again the convent, the court, or the monastic life of the past. They will link together in the spirit, they will like to be together in companionship. Not only will they meet within their Sanctuary or Temple but they will desire to meet socially outside and to spend certain periods of time in the open air together, that they may contact God through the Deva kingdom.

Every five-hundred-year incarnational period is of course a preparation for a much greater and more important incarnational period still, and that is the period which comes at the end of an epoch of two thousand years. That is time as you understand it, we do not use time in the world of spirit in the same way. Think of it as phases of the Moon and also of the wind and the Equinox.

The important part of these really majestic incarnational cycles lies in three different directions. First of all, the student with spiritual knowledge is called upon to go out into the highways and the hedges, to bring in to the Marriage Feast all men and women who appear to be outside the Sanctuary but who played their parts at the end of the previous epoch. Therefore, there will be a great coming together of the past, the incarnations of the past, and these will be linked, with love and understanding by those who are incarnate in the present, with the work as going forward for the New Age. Therefore, they will be looking forward into the future to see where among the souls that they contact are souls which are

52

here merely to prepare for a next and important incarnation under the new Christ. They will therefore be looking backwards, they will look at the present, learn all about the present and they will look to the future.

The future at the present period concerns the Age of Aquarius and the coming of a new Christ whose task it is to teach you to transmute your physical body into light.

So now, in this incarnational period, which is the period of preparation for the New Age, we find large numbers of souls incarnate to clear and cleanse not so much their own personal karma but the karma of the Temple of the past, a Temple which should never have been touched by darkness. Temples must be cleansed through every etheric plane until the Glory of God alone shines within them. Just as you reach out and unfold your consciousness on first one plane and then another higher than the last, so you are to do the same with your physical body, cleansing and purifying every part of that body until the glandular system and the organs and the bloodstream are full of light, so full of light that no darkness can enter, for there is no place for it.

In this you are playing a very important and also a very great part, for many who are incarnated to day have been present at one time or another at those ugly blood sacrifices in the Temples to which they belonged. Those who were present were taking part either mentally or physically in those blood sacrifices and in that taking part were definitely making themselves liable for cleansing.

That is what you have come to do now, to cleanse yourselves, to purify your bodies through every organ, every cell, every system, and through that purification give passage to the light, that the light may transmute everything which is left after your cleansing into light and may become light and be of light.

This is very hard work. You will probably find that walking beside you in this work are many who are quite unconscious of the part they play but are taking just as important a part in the cleansing as you are. There are those in the realm of sound who have to cleanse and purify the ether of the ugly sounds of the dark

53

Temples, which have come back in such large quantity into the dance halls and the material places of amusement.

This must be done through all planes of consciousness and it must be done by souls in the physical body who can be perfect channels for the light.

Those who reincarnate at the end and the beginning of a period — the end of one period and the beginning of another period — are of course given great gifts of vision and hearing, of smell and intuition and touch. Therefore, they are called to fulfil a purpose in the world of men which is important, and part of that purpose is that they may become channels for the glory of light which is to be projected when our Father-Mother God calls for it from the great Deva or Angels. These Deva are dependent upon lesser Deva in every plane of consciousness between their own plane and your earth plane for your help in the production of sound and light and colour through the human bodies of those who are the light-bearers of the new Christ.

They are pioneers. They are undertaking work which has never been done in their knowledge before, because the Christ of Aquarius is a totally different Christ from any Christ force which has manifested before. The power that comes with that incoming Christ is of very great moment to our Father-Mother God and to all those souls who, over the ages, have striven to obey His law and to purify their souls in His service, that they may return to Him clad in His promise of Peace.

You are living in a period of confusion and turmoil, of accidents and death. These things must happen before the light can break, for the old order must change and the new order must manifest. You face wars, that man may learn through the horrors of war the glories of peace and bring peace within your own heart and within the heart of all you touch so that the light of that peace may radiate and bring peace in the world.

You cannot order peace. You can order men to stop fighting physically, but if they have not completed their battle they will return in private to complete it. They must turn their hearts to the light so that as individuals they become a mighty band of light-bearers, to carry the Peace of God with them.

Everything in life seems to be reaching crisis point. Scientific inventions call man to power, yet he must learn to use that power according to the will of God before those inventions will belong to God. The brains of mankind, which are the physical portion of the mental make-up of man, are being strained and strained until there is no use left in them; they have reached crisis point and they will break. In complete reversal of the order of academic achievement, you find a far greater number of apparently useless individuals, useless because they do not possess the power to use their brains and their physical bodies to full capacity.

So you have these heavily weighted scales. Brilliant men and women weighing down the scale till it touches the floor. That cannot be because there must be balance in life, therefore weakness both physically and mentally must manifest in the other scale until that touches the floor, and then into the centre of that will come light which will merge and transmute both into light.

Some are creating karma as they go along: very often day by day, month by month and certainly a definite amount each year. But if you keep your Festivals rightly, that is the time when you come to show gratitude and to give praise to the great angelic Beings who come to help you because you are among those who prepare the way for the new Christ. That power from the Holy Angels will strengthen you; it will create you anew, it will help you to continue the work which you have come to do for the Father-Mother God. Above all, it will bring you sufficient light to clear your karmic debt by the illumination which it will pour through your mind to show you where you have made mistakes.

It will bring sufficient light to clear those karmic conditions which we have created and which were created as we went along day by day and which are, with God's help, permitted to fall away from us that we may not carry them forward. We shall lose some of our light in clearing them, but if we can clear them in this life, how far we shall go when we cross the bridge of death into the next.

8. *The Pattern of Life*

We need to become conscious of the pattern of life. We are content occasionally to accept the words: 'None came into his place by accident; it is the very place God meant for thee', and to take that word 'thee' as meaning our own personal selves. It has a very much wider meaning than that, and we have much to learn in order that we may use the knowledge in connection with our work which lies in the world of men, among so many people.

When a man sets to work to make an instrument he needs certain parts which must be shaped and prepared according to certain measurements. The great turbine demands enormous material to make it and put it together and yet it depends upon every single tiny cog and point being in its right place and rightly adjusted so that it can be run without friction.

So is it with life. Every tiny detail of the life of man, and of humanity, is planned and put together in the planes of light, and put together in such a way that if it depended only upon that etheric pattern, the instrument of life would run very smoothly indeed. There would be no jarring notes, no broken cogs, no wheels moving out of rhythm with the whole rhythm of the machine; all would be harmony as it is in the etheric places, before the pattern is copied and built upon earth.

Each one of you belongs to that vast plan, and each one of you has your own place which has been prepared for you from the beginning of time, when you, a child of the Breath, were launched for the first time into the ethers of light to learn about God, before you came to take up an incarnation in the body of flesh as a child of man.

Your soul was different from every other soul which you met and it is still different today – as different as are your features, as different as your touch and your voice and your feelings, from every other person whom you meet in life. That soul was an extremely beautiful thing. It was a creature of God, created child of the Breath, of light moved by colour and sound dependent upon vibration, and with many powers wonderfully developed for use in those etheric worlds.

But you do not take a child and segregate him in a beautiful spot where no harm or darkness, or even the greyness of twilight, can touch him. Though you shield him in his babyhood, he must learn certain lessons, that he may grow strong and go out among his fellowmen as a being of God infused with the light and the love of God and enfolded in His power, His strength and His truth.

When that moment comes for him to leave your side, he must be strong with all the knowledge that you are able to give him, and you will plant his feet firmly on the ground that he may look at his companions with love and understanding and not shrink from his trials and difficulties, for you have prepared him for them and told him how to act.

In this, you are in a sense copying the example of our Father-Mother God in His handling of you as a child of the Breath. Then, you dwelled in the sheltered glory of that heavenly plane, surrounded with light, having learned to praise your Father-Mother God, having learned to bring Him your offering of thanksgiving and having learned that one day you would be called upon to descend through those planes of light to a plane of density where you would be imprisoned in a physical body and learn to find your way alone, even as the child whose tender first steps you have watched must step away from you when the times comes for him to do so.

That preparation of light and colour and sound, and above all, of

58

truth, was a very fine preparation for your coming forward. It gave you strength, it gave you vision and it gave you above all an armour of light with which you could avert all that came towards you that you would know and feel immediately was not of God. Perhaps it was a little unfortunate that you had to come down through those many planes to the earth plane, that you had to suffer birth and death in first one plane and then another plane until eventually you came to the moment of birth when you entered the physical body and took your place in life.

First of all we realise the glory and the beauty of that Atlantean life which was granted to us, of the spacious gardens and forests where the sunlight was strong and the glory of God moved within it, and where there was, for our service, a glorious Temple, iridescent and shining. In it we found peace and strength and understanding, and here we met for the first time in the flesh those whom we must meet again and again and again as we return to earth to reincarnate into different circumstances. This we must do that each life might teach us one lesson which would help us to help humanity when the time came for us to draw near to the earth as discarnate souls and to bring to our Father-Mother God knowledge of earth's conditions that He might prepare light to shed in the darkness, that the darkness might be overshadowed and taken away.

From Atlantis there were other incarnations in which we touched men who had sinned, and it was perhaps our duty to help that sinner to find the faith again. Perhaps in an incarnation in Egypt we have misused the power which was given to us in that place of position. Perhaps we have not listened to the voice of God; perhaps we have grown too far from those lessons of truth which were given to us in the great and glorious Temple of our being, too far to remember them and have found a greater pleasure in the things of the world, and so we have become worldly. All the time, beside us, are walking those who served with us in that great Temple. Some have more light than we have, some have less; we meet them in sleep and we know why we have come to earth; yet we separate instead of keeping together, a mighty band of light and truth; we separate and go our several ways, cast God aside and try to forget Him in the joys of the material world and the pleasures of material life.

Then our next life would have been chosen for us as a means whereby we might regain grace from which we had fallen, through meditation and concentration, and we have perhaps stepped aside from the world altogether, entering the cloistered precincts of the monastery or the convent. If we wished to achieve complete silence towards the world we would have chosen a Silent Order in which the power of speech is not used. In that convent life, or monastic life, we will have learned many lessons which we would give the world to know and understand today. We will have learned to release the etheric body that it may journey to the place of light. We will have learned to enjoy the glory of Nature. We will have come up against only people who were living the same life as we were, the life of prayer and thanksgiving, creeping down stone stairways in the early hours of the morning at the summons of a bell.

Why does that bell today ring such a harsh note on your ear? Were you restive in that convent life because it called you from the pleasant dreams of the etheric places you left, back into a world which presented cold, hard comfort to you who were of the Spirit? Did you withdraw more and more into yourself? It was a life of sacrifice to a large extent, but not entirely, for it was what you wanted to do; you have chosen that way of life, and therefore, were not allowed any deep psychological understanding of your fellowmen. They were all of the same pattern as you were, and as you looked at them and realised how different you were from them, and they from you, you longed for a wider field of labour, but remember, always you were meeting those same friends and labourers and servants whom you met in the great Temple of Light.

You were protected and sheltered and you had no responsibilities, and when in your next life it was made necessary for you to return to a life of responsibility, with what apprehension you faced it! But you were beginning to see more clearly that life in the convent and the monastery, withdrawn in the silence of Nature and God, had set the seal of its discipline upon you, and there was much in the world of men which you would adjust to the pattern of the convent and the monastery.

How you longed to retreat from the crowds and the noise! It would be very difficult for you to take an entirely material life after such a life of quiet and peace, but what vision you had! You are beginning to see why you are on earth and to realise that you must keep your feet very firmly on the path in front of you, treading step by step forward, not stepping aside to pick flowers, not stepping aside to bathe in the cool waters of the lake, but bearing the burden and the heat of the day. For if you step aside for the joys which are not meant to be yours in this day of time, you are leaving an empty place which no one else can fill and which can cause others to stumble, for they will not expect it to be there.

It is that companionship of life that has grown round out of all knowledge from your beginning. This time you have returned not only to meet all those who knew you in the solitary place of the convent or the monastery, not only to meet those who fought the cause of peace in distant lands beside you, not only to meet those discoverers and explorers come now in very humble places to what they held before, but to meet a mighty army of men and women who for you bear not the stamp of God at all. But think of the privilege that is granted you. The privilege of teaching these souls who know not God, showing them the way of truth and uplifting them towards the light, showing them the path of peace and their place in life.

In your daily task and your daily ministry you are finding yourselves up against unusual problems. You are teaching these natures of the life-spark which you find hard to understand, and you realise that in making the contact with them you are touching a lack of balance, for the child of the Breath has achieved balance through many lives. In that lack of balance you are touching an aggressive feature which was not there before. You may say that it is due to the Communist element in your midst; you may give it all sorts of names, but in your heart you know that it is because there are mingling in the world today men whose only thought is for power and aggrandisement for themselves. These men have children; they say: 'the children are mine', and you know that they are only lent to them that they may set their feet upon the path of strength and knowledge. Yet you must walk beside them, for the links of the children of the Breath have been spread wide abroad, that between them there may be places which will be filled by the children of the life-spark.

It is difficult to teach them that they must walk in the straight path also, and that if they fall aside from that path others will suffer. They will not care for their suffering. It is for you, with that greater light and that greater knowledge gained in all these wonderful incarnational lives which you have touched, to teach them the way.

And yourself? You have not completed your own lessons, otherwise you would be feeling quite differently towards mankind. You are looking at the great cycle of humanity today and you need to realise that, just as every cog in the great machine is slightly different in size and yet the machine depends upon the running of every wheel, so you are looking at a vast machine of life in which the aggression which appears at the top will appear at the bottom also. The aggression which appears among nations will appear in companies and communities and among individuals, because there is a great power working. It is the power which is setting in motion a new machine of a different order and different calibre, a different construction. Because the machine cannot be eliminated wholly to make place for the new one, each little wheel and cog and point and screw must be replaced as we go forward.

So every day in the life of the Aquarian counts, because every day he must cast something away and put something new in its place. He must realise his place in that great Cosmic scheme of life, for our Father-Mother God watches always and you are of importance to him. So is the soul of the murderer and the thief and the blackguard, just as important as you are, but in a different way. You must realise that in your own little family life you are working out one portion of that great plan of life which is mirrored for you and for those who guide you, and for all who contact you, as a vast incarnational cycle. Outside your family you touch your clubs, your schools, your colleges, and at the same moment as the disharmony occurs in your own home by your own fireside, the disharmony must touch that wider circle of life which surrounds you and links with you, because you are part of it. Every angry word is mirrored not only in your own soul and in your home, but in the larger communities which are dependent upon you, and every angry word is mirrored as an act of aggression in the greater world which man commands today. At least he commands it, but God watches, and God holds the rays which direct the feet of the world. If that angry word in your home is going to cause unhappiness which will create a karmic condition which you and others must come back again to clear, then you must suffer in this life for the use of that angry word, or fury, or temper, or jealousy, whatever it is.

But do remember this, that every thought of your own is picked up by every star and planet in the firmament of heaven, and if that happens, that thought must touch all that lies between the earth and the star. Use love, use light, use truth to cancel anger, that long before the word of anger or the thought of jealousy has reached the Iron Belt, it will be completely killed by the glory of the love and the truth which you send out to follow it.

If war comes there will be all sorts of people who will be blamed for it, but those who work with you from the world of spirit know that every lie, every angry word, every deceit, every act of jealousy, has played its part in that vast cosmic set-up. For, when you come to earth in the body of flesh, you meet those two great forces – the forces of Lucifer and the forces of Ahriman. The forces of Lucifer which seek to capture all that touches the ether and push it back into the earth itself, and the forces of Ahriman which seek to turn light into darkness.

63

It is the war between these two, Lucifer and Ahriman, which causes confusion, and that confusion must always occur when the power, or the light of God has been withdrawn. And you will watch that. In various places the light has had to be withdrawn, for a greater light was needed in another place in order to build light, and when the power or light of God is withdrawn, it is never withdrawn unless the person from whom it is withdrawn, or who is the channel for the light, wishes its withdrawal.

We must guard ourselves not only for the sake of our own work as individuals, but above all for the sake of those who walk beside us on the path of life.

9.   *The Bowl of the Potter*

Those who have studied even a little of the writings of Confucius will find continual mention of the key, and if you look for the meaning which Confucius attaches to the key, you will find that the key of which he speaks is the moulding of the personality. The moulding of the personality is indeed, as he says, the key to life. For man has come on earth to mould his personality into the shape and form of God. God gave him his soul, and his soul depends upon the personality linking with the soul to become one with God. It is your personality which will be remembered when you leave the body behind and go to that place of light to complete your life with God, and it is the personality which you will be expected to manifest when you return to earth from time to time to guide and direct those whom you have left behind.

Among those whom you will leave behind, there will be some who will have known you in the flesh and who, although they will have revered and loved the soul within you, will remember really the personality. So you must be able to manifest that personality to them if they are to carry out your instructions and your desires for the fulfilment of your work because, above all, your work does not end with death. Your life in the world of men is but a preparation for that greater life beyond, and in the moulding of your personality you are not only living as God wants you to live and desires you to live, but you are preparing for the change called death, that you will be able to take your place in the Great Unseen, and be seen of men because of the light which you carry.

Among the many Eastern symbols that are given continually by Eastern Philosophers is the Potter at his Wheel, and he is always making and moulding the same article. It is a bowl. He forms the shape and he presses it and moulds it on the wheel, and he uses his tools to smooth it, and when it is completed it is empty within, and that is the symbol of man. For the whole glory of man lies in that emptiness within, which is inhabited by God, from whom all life and all light comes.

Your personality is a strange thing, it is a cleansing and purifying agent for your soul, for your inner self. You may think that if you dwell in thought upon your personality that you are becoming egotistical, but you will never be an egotist in that connection if you can remember that self-abnegation is one of the great parts of that work in the moulding of your personality.

When you set off from that place of light where you dwelt with God, you had returned after many incarnations and offered your soul, scarred by the battles of life, and offered to God too, your wisdom which you had gained. God regarded you, and perhaps He saw that you had won, perhaps He saw that you had failed, but He did not look either at the winning or the losing, He looked at the way you had overcome life. It may have been that the path which you planned was an extremely difficult one, that you gave your personality very little chance of developing the God-like form you hoped it would have, but He did not look at that either. He merely looked at that inner you, which showed Him how you had carried His love and His light in the world of men – whether you had returned beaten down and broken by the experiences you had set yourself, or whether you had returned triumphant, ready, after a certain purification, to return to earth to complete those experiences by moulding yet another personality, that you might offer another empty bowl of a greater glory, at the foot of the Throne.

You, who are Children of the Light, have come to earth with great gifts, and whether those gifts will show and stand you in good

66

stead depends entirely on how you handle your personality. You have been given so much help before you came, for the stars and the planets have come to your assistance and offered you their guidance, and you have chosen your path and mapped it and planned it, so that you should overcome those weaknesses and not return to God with them again.

This time you have come into a life of a very, very different texture from any life you have touched before. For the first time you are meeting in your daily routine – in your shops and offices and your professional life, in local Government and Politics, in omnibuses and trains in which you travel – hundreds of thousands of Children of the Life Spark. These Children are treading a very difficult path, but an entirely different path from you because they have not the teachings of Jesus in their hearts and they have not studied, nor do they know the meaning and the purpose of His coming to earth.

If you were to visit some of the expensive schools to see whether the boys and girls under eleven are going to be able to take the academic honours which are necessary for them before they can enter the wider school life at the age of thirteen, you would find that of the majority of these children, especially those who are educationally backward because their fathers have served abroad and they have had many changes in their education, there are only one percent, one in every hundred, who know the meaning of the Manger Bed and the Life of Jesus.

Without that knowledge there is no guiding principle for man. Therefore, you are called to mingle with those Children of the Life Spark, to enable your light to shine that they may realise, when they contemplate your life, that you have something different, and you must make that difference pleasant and happy so that they will desire to have it. You will meet jealousy, you are bound to do so, but jealousy is a good thing if it leads them to contact the light, to contact you because you are a light bearer. For not only are you called to purify your soul, as the Eastern teacher calls life the hygiene of the soul, but you are called to shed light on these men and women that they may learn also the meaning of the soul and seek that light. Where they are drawn to that something which you have got and they have not, the soul is already awakening, they are making their first contact with God. If you are called to be a channel to direct the power towards them, use that power in the right way and learn to use it by moulding your own personality until it mirrors the personality of your fellowmen, and see not his shortcomings but his possibilities.

There may be some in whom there is no possibility at all – we are not thinking of criminals and evil-doers of that type, but of the ordinary men and women who form the great mass of the British and international public today. To them the message goes forth. You may come in contact with them in healing, and it is because the healing power is of such vital importance in the world that you are being held back until you have completely moulded your personality to the way of God. Then you will be ready to heal and you will be glad of that long, long wait; you will be glad of the patience you have had to exercise in order to wait for the moment to heal in the way God wants you to. For the healing of tomorrow, the healing of Aquarius, is a gathering together of all men under the light. It is a teaching of those who have fallen away from God, as well as of those who know not God. You may read their hearts by the subjugation of pain and life, and leave the imprint of your light on their brow.

The culture of the East has much to teach us, and the time has come to amalgamate East and West. From time to time we shall pause for a moment and look back at the men who lived and served with Jesus. There were some who walked beside Him from boyhood, from the very beginning of His Ministry, and who learnt through that closeness and that friendship and that brotherhood, to turn the other cheek when they were derided as His followers. But these men knew that, when He had been called to manifest life after death to all men and had returned to His Father, the treasures which He left them on the earth must be defended and that it was no longer the right time to turn the other cheek but to stand up for the truth which He had left.

That was how the Christian Church was formed, because the men who had walked beside Him knew their mission. He had taught them to mould their personalities in the mirror of God and He left them with the promise that if they formed that church on the Great Rock called Peter, He would be with them all the day long and through the darkness of the night. He left them the Cup which He had used at the Last Supper, and they knew that they must defend that Cup with their lives because it was proof that He had been with them. Time and time again, those who wanted to destroy the Christian Church endeavoured to seize the Cup and trample it into the dust. They would not allow it, they preferred rather to be smitten to the death. The very man who turned his right cheek to the zealot who had smitten him when he walked beside the Master, and had turned the other cheek also while the Master was with him, knew that once the Master had ascended to His Father there must be no more turning of the other cheek because He had left His power with them.

If you study the Eastern people, the cultured people and the scholars, you will find that their courtesy is entirely impersonal. You will meet many men and women who have dwelt in the East with very little understanding of their culture, who will say they are covering up something. It is a surface courtesy which means nothing, but the Eastern Teacher never allows any man to look within his soul. The personality is the outward sign of the soul and his whole endeavour is to draw the light of the soul through the personality so that the personality stands impersonal and Godlike in the midst of the people.

You who must journey into the world in the midst of these Children of the Life Spark, must learn to unfold and mould your personality so that it becomes completely impersonal, so that you are not hurt by the catastrophes which alarm other people. You know they are incidents which are working according to the Plan of Life under the Will of God. In that complete impersonality towards your fellowmen you will again touch the bowl of the potter, for the virtue of the bowl lies in the emptiness which God can fill. Your impersonality lies as the glory which covers and overshadows the Glory of God within.

Deep down within the heart of the Eastern Teacher the Plan is moulded and prepared, not only just for the span of life in the physical body which he is facing now, but for that preparation which enables him to pass through the gates of death without fear and to know what lies beyond. It enables him to use the power of God in the defence of his laws and to realise that, though the personality is all that is seen by the man in the street, the soul which belongs to God holds the love of God and may not be turned aside by any man who would seek to seize it and trample it in the dust.

For we find in the writings and teachings of Confucius poured out for all men, that the key to life lies in the moulding of the personality.

10. Vibration – Its Relation to Sound and Colour

I

The question of vibration is vast. It rings like a bell, and yet there are so many who use that word 'vibration' about the common little incidents of everyday life. To many it means simply something which oscillates or moves, but it means very much more than that.

From the personal angle, vibration is your note. It is the note which you strike in the world of men. It is the note which rings through the ethers of the astral world. It is the note which rings in the Garden of Remembrance, and the note which rings in the plane from which you came, through many planes of light, to come into incarnation, created children of the Breath. For you were created upon that vibrational note of golden light which breathed into you the Breath of Life, which gave to you the living note which links you with your Father-Mother God, and which links you for all time with your affinity or twin-soul.

Every movement you make displaces the ether. It may be a step upon a hard pavement, it may be a movement of your hand or arm, it may be a flash of joy from the eyes, or the smile from lips which greet you. Each one of these minute movements, of which you make hundreds every day, are definitely your vibration. You can never use anyone else's vibration. Your vibration belongs to you

71

from the beginning of time to the moment when you have completed your work for God and are reabsorbed into the great Cosmic Light, which is God.

Your vibration can be of many textures, many colours, many lights. It can link you with the darkest moment in hell; it can link you with the friends who come to meet you after death in the Garden of Remembrance; it can link you in the hour of sleep with those who journey beside you to the plane to which you belong, where your work is undertaken in the spirit. It can link you through many planes of consciousness beyond and above the Garden of Remembrance to your own archetype, to your own twin-soul, and to your own higher self, and through these three it can link you with God.

When you pray, you set in motion the vibration of love. If you pray for yourself, for the means to enjoy power, material greatness and material wealth, as many, many people do, your vibration will be dark. It will sound no note of light to anyone who seeks to guide you, nor very frequently to anyone who loves you on the other side of life. It will attract towards you myriads of discarnate souls, who wander disconsolate about the earth plane desiring to function from time to time through a mind incarnate in the physical body. Therein lies one of the great dangers of Spiritualism, on the lower level, because it is your own desires set out on a dark vibration, attracting their like from the astral world, that causes a very great many of the cases of obsession, or possession, or dual personality.

But if you pray for yourself that you may lead a good pure life, that you may be prepared for God's service, that you may see the light through the darkness of evil, if you hold your hands out and offer yourself to God, asking that He shall use you as it seemeth best to Him, that prayer sets in motion a vibration of light and colour. To those who guide you it is a note of quivering power, and they come towards you in order that they may drink in every word of your prayer, and give back the power which you have given for them to approach you. That is vibration in prayer where you are concerned, and they can carry that prayer through the many, many channels through which it must pass, before it becomes the glory of light which God can give back to you as the gift of strength and purity and peace. But it must go through those channels to God, because it is a prayer for yourself, and you are setting in motion your own vibration upon the ether of light.

When you pray for others, when you set aside yourself and your own desire to do God's work which, great though it is, is less than your desire for others to do God's work, that sets in motion a vibration of light and colour which is staggering in its power and speed — for we must remember that vibration works upon light, upon colour, upon sound and upon speed — and that prayer goes direct to God.

If you were a creature without vibration, without the power to project light into the heavens, that prayer could never reach God, for it is vibration which is your link with Him. Although, if it were a vibration of darkness which coloured your prayer for others, there would be many hands and many minds to build a door to prevent its passage to the worlds of light. But because that prayer is light for others, desire for others' good and strength and power, that vibration speeds its way to God. It is God alone who can give power to that vibration to return, and when it returns, it does not return to you. It returns on another note altogether, to the soul that is in need of your help and for whom you have prayed.

Our note of vibration can be pure only when our heart is pure. If we act wrongfully towards our fellowmen, if we desire gain for ourselves, that vibration can never reach beyond the great iron curtain which surrounds and separates earth from heaven. Why is it that the work of some healers in prayer healing, or absent healing, is so much stronger or much more powerful than others? If we are talking of the things of the spirit, it is because their vibration is pure. Vibration is power. Whether it is power for good or power for evil depends entirely on you yourself, and on your desire and understanding of its use.

Within the physical body we have that tenuous, glorious etheric body — the etheric body whose maladjustment is the cause of so

73

much sickness in the world today. You cannot go very far, whether you are teaching or healing or just living the lives of ordinary people, without understanding the etheric body.

Within the etheric body are seven centres. Each one of these centres governs its own colour, and wherever there is colour there is vibration. Therefore, each centre responds to its own vibration, its own colour, its own sound. To be perfectly tuned in to the vibration of the whole body, these centres must be tuned in perfect harmony with each other, and the harmony, the tuning place of the seven chakra or psychic centres is the centre at the base of the spine, and that centre governs Kundalini. That is why it is so dangerous when you first begin development to hasten it, for in hastening it you raise Kundalini. And in hastening the rising of Kundalini, you spoil your light, your colour, your sound, with darkness.

Each etheric centre, each chakra, must be perfectly in harmony with that main vibration within the spine, which is you. Why is that harmony necessary? Because only when you are entirely rhythmically tuned in to the plane to which you belong, can you link in with your twin soul, either on earth or in heaven, or can you hear the note of your archetype, or can you hear intuitively the Voice of God. For when God speaks He makes no mistakes. He does not speak to Mr. Jones' vibration when He really intends to send a message to Mrs. Smith. He knows the sound, the colour, the light, and that vibration which is you, and the road to you from heaven to earth is clear, so that His Voice can be heard along that line.

Vibration is an individual and personal thing. It belongs to your soul, and during your life on earth it belongs to your personality. It is the signature tune of the real you, and if it is strong, then you are pure and strong and good. If it is weak in sound and colour and light, then there are things in your life which need adjustment and alteration. If you are selfish, the note will be feeble to such an extent of feebleness that those who guide you will have great difficulty in understanding it.

74

Vibration – its relation to Sound and Colour

If you are jealous, that will frequently cut off your vibration altogether, so that it cannot penetrate beyond the astral plane at all. That is one of the reasons why it is so tremendously important that the lives of old people who are likely to be nearing the world of spirit, day by day travelling rapidly towards the gate of death, should be taught by all who know and understand these things, that jealousy and selfishness can bar their way to the light. Not only can it cut out the power of healing, which will strengthen them and make them more fit and more able to fulfil those last years on earth, but it can dim their pathway for a long, long time once they have passed through the gate of death. For a vibration which is soiled by selfishness and jealousy needs a very, very long time for cleansing and purification.

Why, as we get older, do we become so difficult? It is because life is slipping away from us, and we know that we must ourselves desire to see ourselves as God sees us. That is a moment for cleansing and purifying our vibration, so that the light can penetrate from God towards us, and from us to God.

For many, many years these things have been held in the darkness of misunderstanding. Now the word of God has gone out: 'Feed my flock. Feed them with knowledge, strength and light, that they may know what life is like on the other side and slowly prepare their own etheric bodies for harmony of their vibration, for the day when there will be no death on this earth at all'.

The preparations going on within ourselves are not for this life alone, but to give an understanding of vibration, that we will be able to handle it and use it.

You would not dream of putting a tool into the hand of a child with an open electric wire in his other hand, nor does God place such dangers in the way of His children. He says: 'Teach my children what is light'. Light is colour, light is sound, but above light, love is the individual vibration of the human soul.

II

The purpose of this teaching on vibration is really to impress upon every single living soul the importance of vibration in life. Every thought of yours has an effect on every single star. If you look up at the heavens on a starlight night, you cannot count the thousands of stars in the firmament of heaven, and yet every act and every thought of yours either dims or strengthens the light in each of those stars.

Man is a very important being, because he comes to earth linked with the world of spirit in such a wonderful way. When we realise that the whole of life is vibration, and that the only difference between a block of wood on which one's hand rests and the light which hangs above one's head is a rate of vibration, we shall realise what great understanding we need to fathom the meaning of the word.

Your physical body is built upon a structure of bone. After death the flesh falls away from the bone, those wonderful organs which constitute the working of the human body disappear, and you are left with a thing you call a skeleton, cold to touch, hard, and in some places very brittle. It is something without life or movement, and yet that bony structure is vibration, because it is crystallised spirit.

Vibration is spirit. Each man bears within himself a minute portion of spirit which makes him part of God. The man who treads the path of life with knowledge is he who is able to find the spirit within himself and to make the fullest possible use of it. God is spirit. Spirit is vibration. Vibration is sound, colour, light. Everything which vibrates is part of God, because vibration is spirit, Spirit is God.

The whole of your life, the path you tread, the work you do, your fulfilment in spiritual work, depends upon your understanding of the polarities – the positive and the negative. Positive vibration is light – light, glory, colour – because positive vibration is harmony,

76

and without harmony we cannot have light. Negative vibration is darkness. Darkness is disharmony. The man who treads the dark path is setting himself up against the law of God, which is light. Light cannot be anything but positive. Darkness cannot be anything but negative.

So we realise that in searching within ourselves to find our own power of spirit we touch with delicate fingers a great and mighty force. A force which links us to the whole universe, which links us to God, which binds us to earth, and which we must learn to use and understand. We must recognise truth, because truth is light and truth is ever seeking to surmount the power of darkness, which is negative, but only negative light.

When you meditate, dwell upon the thought that vibration is divided into two parts: the vibration of light, which is positive, and the vibration of darkness, which is negative. You can find positive vibration through all growing things. You can find light below the soil, and in the soil, and in the plant. But you can also find negative vibration, which is destruction, because negative vibration is disharmony, and disharmony is disease.

We have come round in a circle, and that circle has brought us back to the point where ill-health starts. Ill-health starts with a disharmony in vibration, and although in the beginning that disharmony may not be entirely darkness, entirely negative, it can become so unless we are careful.

Every time your fingers touch an inanimate object, that object, although it seems dead to you, draws something from the vibration of your fingers. If you place your hand upon the rail of a bus as you get in, and you are feeling good-tempered, harmonious, pleasant, that vibration is transmitted through your fingers to the bar on which your hand rests. The next person behind you mounting the 'bus, who holds that bar where your hand has rested, can absorb that vibration or reject it. If he absorbs it and you have been harmonious, a thread of harmony will run through his body. He may not be conscious of it, but you have given him healing. You have helped to chase disharmony or darkness from his soul. You have joined a fragment of light to the fragment of the spirit of God which is within him, and created a greater light. Even if that light is no bigger than the flicker of a match, it is light, and light is harmony.

So is it throughout the universe. The thought of harmony that goes forth from your mind is transmitted as light as far as it can reach, and it can reach a very long way. That light will pass through many planes as a tiny, tiny silver arrow. It will touch many discarnate souls; those on the astral plane will probably not feel it at all; those a little further advanced will be conscious of a pleasant sensation; those who are further away, and therefore more spiritual and able to touch the light with a greater strength, will absorb your pin-point of light and grow strong upon it. That is positive vibration, positive strength, positive light, which helps you to fulfil your body in harmony and to cast out the darkness. For every time that a thought of harmony is absorbed into your physical body, it must displace some disharmony, and disharmony is disease.

We hear so much about operations. We hear so much about treatment for disease, and yet, if we could flood our bodies with light there would be no need for these things at all. Sometimes the more treatment we have, the greater our positive vibrations are dimmed, and as they are dimmed, the darkness intervenes and drags us deeper and further away.

We know the tremendous value of the esoteric bloodstream; how that esoteric stream purifies and cleanses the physical bloodstream. That could not be achieved without positive vibration, for positive vibration is strength, life, light. That is why meditation is of such importance to all men, because in meditation you are setting aside the negative vibrations of the material world and drawing yourself within the shadow of the great light of God, which is positive.

Every time you touch vibration, you touch light and sound and colour. The touch of your fingers on the rail of the 'bus can produce notes strong on the ether. Those notes are of the greatest possible value to those who have crossed the bridge of death, because those notes bring a message to them and help them to understand the change in their lives and the change in the world around them. Negative vibration is so cruel, so unlike God, that it is astonishing that it exists at all. The negative vibration which brings disease, the sharp tongue which casts fear into the heart of a friend, the cruel action which makes a man or woman afraid to face life, the insecurity which one man can bring upon another by his mistrust and suspicion, the grasping of material wealth from others who must remain without the necessities of life – these are all vibrations of different rates, different currents. They bring disease, they create disease. For wherever men of that type move, they leave their mark on the door handle, on the handle of the taxicab, on the bar of the 'bus, on the ether which they breathe with you – they leave a darkness which brings fear.

It is such things as these, doubled, trebled, which leave the dark vibrations in empty places that make men afraid. In the past, where the priest had offered the sacrifice of the blood, long after the rituals were completed and the temple emptied and closed, fear and darkness remained – negative vibrations which, like evil ugly beings, caught hold of the shoulders of those who came without much strength in life, and frightened them into subjection to the power of evil.

Crimes like that, and darkness, are also felt throughout the firmament. Through every plane of light, to the most distant star, that negative darkness is felt. If sufficient positive power is not created to kill that darkness, the harm, the damage, that can be done to your fellow man is incredible.

Those are the evils which strike your fellow man through your actions. What about the negative vibration which strikes you yourself down onto a bed of sickness? From the moment that you endeavour to unfold the consciousness, you are expected to cleanse and purify your whole physical body, and your whole etheric body, of negative vibrations. It is a slow process, and sometimes it happens that a number of negative vibrations come together and cause quite a serious condition of fever. We call that a cleansing or clearing of the etheric, and sometimes it is better for us that that

79

cleansing should take place at one moment, even if it keeps us away from work and in bed for twenty-four hours. But that cleansing process is going on the whole time. From the moment that you place your hand within the hand of God, to tread the path with love and understanding, every moment of your day must be spent in casting out the darkness, which is negative vibration. You will find, only when you have completed that task, that your body will be working in harmony, that your soul will be escaping into the realms of sleep in harmony, and that your etheric centres will be moving rhythmically and smoothly in tune with each other, that your own note, your own vibration, will come out on the ether as a thing of light, not darkness.

But there are very few men and women in the world who can look into their own souls and say: 'I am not in the least little bit selfish. I am not given to gossip or backbiting. I am not given to jealousy or unkind remarks. I try to give my fellow man as much as he gives me'.

Every time a jealous thought goes out on the ether, it is a negative vibration which returns to hit you yourself. Every time you remember yourself before someone else, you are being selfcentred, and you are drawing within yourself, not the positive vibration of light, but the negative vibration of darkness, and that will punish you, not your fellow man. Every time that thought of selfishness, that thought of jealousy, is voiced in the spoken word, the strength of the vibration is doubled. For it has become sound, and colour – the sound and colour of jealousy and malice, and they are indeed ugly on the ether.

Endeavour to see the effect in the physical body of yourself and your friends – negative vibration or positive vibration. It is not a virtue to have a cold. It is not a virtue to suffer disease. Rather do we prefer to keep these things to ourselves, and conquer them by drawing more and more light within ourselves, that the light may conquer the darkness, and the vibration of our physical body may no longer be disharmony and disease, but harmony and light. And if we do God's work truly, that will come of itself.

80

Vibration — its relation to Sound and Colour

Except in very exceptional cases, every man who suffers sickness – except where there are unusual karmic conditions – can cure that disease by understanding positive vibration. That is what the work of the analyst is today. It is bringing to the surface the darkness and drawing it away, and it is placing in its place positive vibration, which will bring strength. But it cannot be done by word of mouth alone. It must be done through the etheric body and the seven etheric centres.

The emptying of the subconscious mind can be a very dangerous thing if it is undertaken without some knowledge of vibration, and some ability to place into that emptiness, when the darkness is removed, light, and to give that soul a way of life on to which he can hold with strength, and cast out disease. This does not refer to serious mental cases, nor karmic conditions. But in nearly all normal cases, disease which is disharmony can be entirely cured by the right understanding of vibration – positive vibration, which is light.

III

Vibration is the force that rules our lives. Without perfect at-one-ment with God we cannot possibly hope to achieve good health, good fortune, or even to tread the path which we have chosen to tread, because only when we are entirely in tune with God can we see the way. Only when we are entirely in tune with God are we in harmony, and harmony allows no room for disease. Harmony fills the soul. It also sees that there is no darkness in the physical body, but that the spirit of God can descend and rise and enfold us with harmony and love, which are wisdom.

Faith is love, but wisdom is love in action, and if we realise that to have faith we must be in tune with the universe, we will realise how much more strongly must we be in tune to have wisdom. That is why wisdom seems so very far away from man, but a time is coming when man will be given more assistance than he has ever had. That assistance will come from the world of spirit, in order that he may attune his soul to God, and attune his soul to his physical body and light. When that is complete the vibration of man with God will be perfect.

We realise that when the soul is destined to come to earth for incarnation, certain spiritual laws must be adopted and worked out to their fulfilment. Some of the planes from which the men and women of today have come are a long distance away from the earth plane. Therefore, the plans for the birth of a child who has a message to bring to earth from the plane to which he belongs, and through that plane from his Father-Mother God, these plans must be made a long, long time before the child comes to earth.

The child chooses his parents under guidance, and sometimes those parents are still in the spirit world when they are chosen. They may already be existing on a high plane of consciousness, or they may be on an astral plane very close to the earth. That depends upon the plan of life prepared for the soul, the experiences which the soul must undertake. When we consider that the child and parents-to-be frequently come together with that understanding before the parents are born on the earth plane, we must realise the tremendous importance of all connected with that birth. The unity, the harmony, the power. But unity can only be achieved if vibration is studied and understood. For these souls who come to earth as the parents, must also have parents who have chosen them, or whom they have chosen, and the vibration through the two generations must be all that is expected for the child who is of any importance on the earth plane today or tomorrow, or whenever he has to come.

Once the parents of a special soul have been chosen, all has to be prepared for the coming of that soul. The parents must take their vibration from the soul who is to be their child. It is not always a positive vibration. Sometimes the child is forced to incarnate into a family where it will mean great misunderstanding and disharmony. But the mere fact that it is born into that family is sufficient for the parents to have to submit to a certain adaptation of their own vibration, in order that they may prepare for the incoming child.

If the home is an inharmonious one to the child, it usually means, but not always, that the parents are on a negative vibration whereas the child is on a positive one, and no soul who is chosen for any special work will ever come to earth on a negative vibration. He may have to learn to overcome negative vibration and to achieve balance. But he himself will be on a positive, clear vibration, a sound which will ring on the ether, a colour which will be projected upon the ether, if he has work to do which our Father-Mother God knows is important.

The plan of the life of the soul is very interesting, because parents and child-to-be must go through a certain education in the plane on which the child's soul functions, in preparation for the earth life. When the time comes for the child to come to earth, all will be arranged according to the signs and the planets under which he is to be born. All these vibrations will be tuned in to light and colour and sound, which will bring him to earth with harmony. He has a long journey to make, this soul. He must come down through many planes before he touches the earth plane, and he sheds a great deal of his light in that descent by adopting a cloak of ether, slightly denser than the previous one, in each plane through which he passes. But however dense is that etheric cloak, however dark is the astral one before he enters the earth, the vibration will always be the same. His archetypal note, his note upon the ether, his light, his colour, will all be synchronised into one perfect unity. So that, from the time he leaves the plane to which he belongs until the moment comes when he lies in the cradle, a tiny weeping creature, the vibration will be identical and his links through each of those planes through which he passed will be strengthened by his power.

It sounds, at the birth of a child, as if he had brought disharmony with him, for he weeps – but do not consider it as weeping. The weeping of a child is not sorrow. It is a cry, and the cry is the ringing of the sound on the ether. No two children who were ever born cry with the same sound. In the same way, no two children ever touch the same vibration closely, except the twin soul and those who are sent to earth, sometimes many countries divided from one another, with a similar mission to fulfil. Therefore the cry of the child is the signal in the material world of the coming into life of another spiritual being, who announces his coming by ringing his own vibration upon the ether, and that vibration is the breath.

The breath has one pulse; the bloodstream has four pulses; and it is at the moment of birth that breath and blood vibration are co-ordinated for their journey into life. For unless the rhythm of the blood and the rhythm of the breath are identical, the health of the child will be precarious and physical life will present mental and physical difficulties of untold rigour.

Many times at the beginning of life, either through mishandling at birth or other reasons, the breath and the blood vibration are not at-one-ed quite quickly enough, and then you will find some trouble which usually affects the valves of the heart. Therefore, where a soul born into the physical body suffers from birth from some valvular weakness, it is usually due to the lack of unity between the rhythm or the vibration of blood and breath.

Those of you who treat the sick, especially the sick who have suffered with heart diseases, will find that if you can readjust the rhythm of the etheric body with the physical, in many cases the disease lessens and the condition of the heart improves. The child born with valvular weakness will frequently, if brought up under the right conditions of sunlight and fresh air, pure food, routine and regular discipline, lose the trouble at the age of seven or fourteen years, because through that way of life planned for the child, the rhythm of the breath and the blood stream are adjusted.

This adjustment of the rhythm of life is a very important matter. You have within your etheric body seven chakra or psychic centres – seven centres which are sensitive to the glorious ethers beyond the normal vision of man. Each one of these centres looks to the clairvoyant like a whirling disc of colour. Each one governs its own particular colour, but the one centre which contains, in addition to the colours of itself, the pure, full, true colour of the vibration of the person, is the centre at the base of the spine.

Vibration — its relation to Sound and Colour

This is not Kundalini, but within your spinal cord there is a minute drop of fluid — fluid so precious that it is of God — and through the vibration of the breath and the bloodstream, the centre at the base of the spine is adjusted to the rhythm of the soul. As that rhythm rises and falls, so does this tiny drop of fluid rise and fall within the spinal column. It is by placing his hand upon the base of the spine of his patient that the healer can find out whether the rhythm, the vibration, is perfect and whether the harmony of the soul is secure within the body.

These seven centres are extraordinarily affected by the vibration of other people, and it is through these centres that you are particularly affected when you say you like or you dislike a person. Sometimes dislikes may be due to a long-forgotten memory of a tiresome incarnation spent together, but far more often it is the little clock on the ether which tells of a cross-current, or cross-vibration in the physical etheric body linking with the soul. These feelings of mistrust or dislike must not be ignored. What we are touching at the moment is vibration, and harmony or disharmony can make or mar your life.

When the rhythm — your own personal particular rhythm, which no one else has or can have — is perfect in the spinal column, your whole body will be in tune. That rhythm affects the great nerve centre at the top of the spine, it affects the centre at the back of the neck where the optic nerve lies, and it affects many of the nerve centres within the head. There is only one organ of the body which can tell you whether that rhythm is in harmony or disharmony, and that is the eyes. Therefore, those who treat patients, will find that a great deal of the diagnosis should be made by looking into the eyes of your patient. Thus can you tell whether the vibration of the soul is harmonious to the body, and whether the rhythm of the body is working in perfect harmony with breath and blood.

The breath and the blood are the two most important parts of man from the spiritual angle, and unless they are in perfect rhythm and perfect harmony it is not possible to have a healthy body. Therefore, in any adjustment that we make, we must realise that a

85

great deal of time must be spent in achieving harmony between breath and blood in our treatment, before we can hope to cure disease.

The rhythm, or vibration, of harmony or disharmony, is projected through the aura of the patient you are treating, or the person to whom you are talking, and it is projected as colour. Not only does the ray on which you have come to earth shine in the aura, but that ray is surrounded by any number of lesser colours which tell the medium whether previous lives have been spent harmoniously or inharmoniously, and whether the soul is sensitive to colour and sound.

Colour is to play an important part in the Aquarian age, and the most dominant note or sound upon the ether, for the Aquarian age, will of course be water. Therefore we must learn to harmonise our vision to the colours of the Aquarian age, and to quicken our hearing to the various hundreds of sounds which different waters emit. You cannot think of vibration as a note which you can strike upon a musical instrument — you can only consider it impersonally as sound. But you must come to know the rhythm of your own body, and the expression in colour and sound of your friends or enemies.

Your aura looks like a great head-dress of feathers, as if a small peacock's tail was fixed at the centre at the back of the neck and stood out all round your head and shoulders. The little hard bit which belongs to every feather — the kind of bone in the centre — denotes the ray on which the child of God has come to earth. It may be red or blue or purple, and the rays of the feathers will show the vibration of the soul. As soon as we see the colour of the vibration of the soul, we know to which plane that soul belongs, and more or less what his previous work on earth has been. Sometimes these feathers are marred or soiled. A grey-green mark across them will show jealousy. If it is a heavy mark it will be jealousy in large proportion, if it is a tiny spot it will be jealousy in small proportion. Ill-temper, anger, love of power — all these negative qualities dim the radiance of the feathers of the aura. It is a

86

very important matter whether these colours dim the feathers, or the feathery part which surrounds the bone, or whether they dim the bone entirely. If they dim the bone entirely, they are cutting the ray on which you have come to earth. When they dim the feathery part only, we know that the disharmony between body and soul can be much more easily cured.

Colour sense should be an important part of the training in the life of every child. The understanding of colour vibration and the joining in harmony of colour, opens the channels for inspiration and intuition. All helpers, all guides and inspirers, who come from the world of light towards the earth plane, are dependent upon the vibration of sound and colour for their descent. If your vibration is weakened they cannot descend with the same speed or the same clarity; if it is strong and rhythmic and perfect in harmony, they can travel swiftly towards you and even the darkness of the astral plane holds no terrors for them.

Every planet, of course, governs its own metal. Therefore, at any time a new planet is discovered, a new metal will also be discovered which belongs to the planet. In other words, each links with that planet, on the vibration of the planet. That vibration is shown upon the ether as strong, vibrant colour.

Recently the planet Uranus has had a very dominant influence upon the life of man. Although his influence is becoming easier, lighter, not so difficult, not so hurtful to the children who are born under strongly his influence, he is nevertheless a tremendous force in the Aquarian age, and the metal which belongs to him is uranium. When Uranus pours out his power, and it is picked up by the metal uranium, the vibration which is set in motion is extremely powerful.

The ray of Uranus is blue, the vibration of that ray is blue. Therefore at the moments when Uranus and the metal uranium link together in perfect harmony and at-onement, there is projected upon the ether of the light planes, or the astral planes (the darker planes) a tremendous force of blue light.

This blue light is like nothing on earth at all. You will find, if you

87

watch, that the necessity for producing this colour, to match the vibration which is being used on the ether, will come to the children of men. In many of the new fabrics, new articles, new inventions, you will find a peculiar blue, which looks as if it has been captured or imprisoned. In the beginning, that blue will be jarring and uncomely, and it will not interest you at all. But gradually you will become accustomed to it, and you will find that your own aura is drawing little by little that blue light into it. That blue ray is of vital importance because it will have such an effect, through its vibration, on the life of man, that many, many things will be completely changed and a greater harmony will come into life through it.

It will take time. It will come first, as all these things do, from the spirit worlds, where only those with clairvoyant vision can touch it, only those who have the gift of etheric hearing can hear it. Then it will make a big drop and it will appear in the material, commercial world. It will appear in fabrics, it will appear in luminous articles, it will appear in plastics, which will immediately be improved in addition. It will appear in many other ways besides, and will gradually adapt itself to the vibration which lies between the higher ethers and the denser ethers. It will become a thing of light, harmony and joy, and you will go out in the morning walking into that vibration, and knowing that you feel good and happy and strong.

That is one only, out of fifty or so, of the new vibrations which are being prepared for the children of men in the Aquarian age. That is coming quickly, and it comes through the linking of Uranus and its metal uranium.

Uranus is the great disintegrating planet which brings catastrophes and things which happen suddenly but, once the suddenness is overcome, brings harmony and peace.

There are two aspects of vibration which would seem very far apart and yet are really very close together. Many thousands of those who used the power of vibration in Atlantis are back in the physical world today, hampered by our difficult physical conditions but nevertheless trying, at all points, to elucidate these ideas which come into their minds from time to time. These ideas are really the awakening of the ancient memory of the past.

Among those hundreds of thousands of souls there are many mediums. The oracles, or mediums, in those great temples of the past used the gifts of clairvoyance, clairaudience and inspiration with a much greater understanding than the majority of the mediums today. They touched the planes of light above the Garden of Remembrance, whereas the majority of mediums today touch only the levels of the astral planes between the earth and the Garden of Remembrance, planes which really, on the whole, have very little to do with God. God guards them, God guides the souls within them, but the power that the medium draws from these planes is choked and darkened as it passes through them. Therefore, the vibration of the original note is lost, and the note which is received is frequently faulty.

The keynote of all vibration is purity – purity of sound, purity of colour. But time, also, has a very great bearing upon vibration on the earth plane. Time – the time sense – can for a psychical person, come to a complete standstill, and the medium, whether he is consciously a medium or not, can find that the vibration of time has stood still for him sometimes a matter of seconds, sometimes a matter of hours.

The medium who works upon a high vibration has a vibration which reaches to and from the planes beyond the Garden of Remembrance; such mediums need an enormous amount of sleep. Contrary to most people in the physical body, the time for the sleep of the medium is from twelve o'clock midnight onwards, until those who have taken the spirit away in sleep call it back. The majority of

89

people in the physical body, who are working at material tasks, have their most refreshing sleep before midnight, but the medium works all through the night. Therefore, the most vital work is fulfilled after the hour of midnight, when the vibrations which are poured from the planes of light, to take the soul-spirit towards them, cannot be contaminated by the dark vibrations of the earth plane. You must remember that all day long you are throwing off matter — you can call it ectoplasm, you can call it power, or vibration — which is influencing the ether in which you move, and is therefore influencing the ether in which others move. If you are feeling cross and unkind, you will affect the vibrations of every soul who passes through that particular portion of the ether where your anger or unkindness have touched.

If you could see an etheric photograph of a group of people sitting in meditation, it would show you, on the fingers, what would look like long Chinese finger-nails. The fingers would have projections. First of all, the finger itself is reproduced on the ether beyond the tip of the ordinary finger, and beyond that again is the vibrant ray of light.

But you have had very much greater power over these rays in the past than you have in the present. Although you know that when death occurs, the body decays and you will not see or use that body again, yet all this power which is being poured into you today, is poured into you for a purpose. Not only for today, not only to awaken the ancient memory of past lives, but in order that you may fulfil your place with power when you return to the world of men in the new age.

For you will have power over the ether. The releasing of the blood is releasing the ethers of the blood. If there is to come a day when, instead of lying down to die, you will slip into the ether and take a journey on the clouds to the Great Beyond, you must be able to use the power of the ether and to control it. You can only do this by studying vibration and by endeavouring to recapture the memory of the past, and through that memory, to learn again how you used this power in Atlantis. Therefore you must go back to the

Source of Light and Life, and to that wonderful land which, for nearly all of you, is represented as a solitary tableland on which stood a great Temple.

Beside that Temple there were mighty forests, wonderful parks and gardens, and beyond these, certainly out of sight of the Temple, was an enormous industrial area. In those days you did not use such a substance as coal. You did not use any of the oil methods of heating, and yet tremendous heat was generated for the moulding of the wonderful metals used in those factories. These metals were moulded with the hands, and they were moulded by the power of vibration which was used through the finger-tips. This vibration was cut off, or increased, according to the power asked for mentally by the workmen. The metals that were used were as sharp and as hard as steel, and yet a man, running his finger down a straight line in the middle of a sheet of metal, could cut that sheet in half.

In these workshops were fabricated the most wonderful flying machines — machines which were controlled by the power of vibration on the ether. The training for those who piloted these machines was long, for it had to be a development of spiritual gifts as well as keen touch and cunning sight. But these birdlike machines in the air were composed of two substances: metal which was moulded by the vibration of the fingers, and these wonderful marbles, or stones, which were entirely plastic. The wings were made of this vivid blue plastic, shining brilliantly in the light like great dragonflies, and these wings were not cut or broken or moulded, in any other way than by the hands of the craftsmen. For according to the rate of vibration of the workmen working on the stone, was the size of the wing, or the density of the colour.

Just as you take a piece of plasticine in your fingers and make it thick or thin, large or small, without taking any of it away, so were these plastic stones moulded, and their durability was extraordinary.

These machines were piloted entirely by vibration, and one day you yourselves will use this wonderful power. In your midst, today, there are many who are endeavouring to put on paper ideas from their heads on these matters. They find themselves fogged and set back, because they are ahead of their time.

But you must learn to master the forces of electricity in this age, and to obtain a knowledge of this power and strength, and watch how each year new forms come into being for which electricity is used. Then indeed you will be able, when you return again, to touch your vibration with knowledge. For your vibration is yours from birth, from the moment that the breath of God breathed into you the breath of life.

That note, on which you said 'Goodbye' to the plane where you were born in the spirit, has been yours untouched for all time. But you can have that vibration cut, and the cutting of your vibration of sound, light and colour, can separate you from God. The only darkness that can cut that vibration is the darkness of Satanaku himself.

11. *The Rays*

I

The man who is able to dowse for water has a certain magnetic quality within himself. This is proved by the fact that the twig or the whalebone turn over when he stands upon a piece of ground underneath which water can be located. Water is sometimes near the surface but it can be very deep underground – so deep that men become discouraged when they try to find it through boring. Boring does not decrease the man's magnetic quality.

The man who uses a pendulum to discover water or oil, or other conditions, has also a magnetic quality of a certain nature. It will be slightly different from the magnetic quality of the man who uses the twig or the whalebone, but it is not any the less valuable for that. These may be material people based upon the physical world, exploring the possibility of the physical world linking with an invisible world, which they have not yet attempted to locate, or which they have attempted to locate without much success.

The man who sets out to cure disease with the pendulum will have an additional quality, because in addition to the magnetic quality of the physical body and the personality of the man himself he must, in order to heal (that is to make whole), have a spiritual quality as well. Therefore, we find within such a man both the psychic, which links with the material, and the spiritual, which links with the invisible worlds of God.

The magnetic quality of physical man links with the Earth only, but when he believes in God and accepts the Power of God in the direction of the world of men, he is opening himself to the spiritual quality of God, which God has placed within him at his birth to be part of his very self. Therefore he is touching – however much we dislike the word – a higher consciousness, a consciousness of Spirit of an invisible power of God which loves and directs the path of man. In order to draw this quality of God towards himself, he must himself be prepared to accept it. He can accept it through the physical body sometimes without giving credence to its power, but in the end he will be forced to accept it through the soul-body, because it is the soul-body which contains the spirit and it is the spirit which is God.

The man who sets out to heal is not looking for material success for himself. He is trying to do something for his fellowman; he is not expecting to heal his own ill-health if he has it, but he is desirous of preventing others from suffering as he does, and he is also desirous of finding out something about the pain and suffering of the world. Therefore he is opening himself to the Power of God, the Invisible. In order to do this he must use the full strength of the psychic foundation which he has built on the magnetic power of God in his own physical body.

The magnetic power is of two qualities: it is of the quality of material man; it is also of the quality of the Spirit. When it holds the power of the Spirit it is extended to the higher consciousness of Spirit which brings that glorious radiance into the physical body of man, to mingle with the magnetic force of the physical body.

Man's physical body functions through the magnetic forces. Every portion of his body, every organ, every nerve, every muscle, is controlled by this magnetic force, and the magnetic force of man is under the guidance or dominance of his will. Therefore, in order to use this magnetic force, he must learn to use his will rightly, and whether he uses that because he knows how to distinguish right from wrong when accepting the physical, or whether he does it while accepting the power and the love of the invisible God, depends upon the man himself. The result of his healing work depends very largely on his attitude of mind towards his power. Some men are very much stronger in material magnetism than others, and others are very much stronger in spiritual magnetism than their fellows who are able to give an enormous force of material magnetism.

Binding these two together we are conscious of Radiation. Radiation means the function of invisible rays; that is the rays which are not visible to the normal physical vision of man. Many people who are magnificent Healers are very fine spiritual workers never see with the physical eye these rays at all, but many more are conscious of rays and of their power, and to many the rays gives forth not only colour and sensation but sound. Therefore, it is of vital importance that we should be very careful in making our foundation entirely spiritual, in order that those rays which we touch are indeed good and of the Love of God, rather than of the Darkness and of the power of Satan.

These rays radiate through the seven chakra of the etheric body, which is the exact counterpart of your physical body. There are many psychic centres or chakra within the etheric body. These chakra move with incredible rapidity within the physical and etheric bodies, and as they absorb unsatisfactory radiation from the physical body they cast it out through the etheric body, into the aura. As they absorb wrong vibrations from the outside, these vibrations or rays are passed through the aura and the etheric body into the physical body where they are frequently the cause of serious disease.

The majority of people with whom you travel and whom you meet are unconscious of the etheric body at all, but you will be conscious of it. You know the power of these radiating chakra and that your physical body is cleansed in sleep by the power of the chakra which you carry and that that cleansing must be completed by spiritual power which is poured through the aura, through the etheric body into the physical body. These unsatisfactory

95

radiations can be passed off through the etheric body or through the physical body when the etheric body is not strong enough to assist in their passage, and therefore they become blocks in the etheric body. Those blocks prevent the Light from entering.

Here we come to the main origin of disease. It is the condition of the etheric body which causes disease in the physical; it is the friction of the etheric body upon the physical and the physical upon the etheric which cause mental illness. Mental illness is frequently the result of a desire for power or dominance in some form or another, or of too great a projection of the will in one's own service instead of in the service of God.

These radiations belong to the personality, and the personality comes to Earth in order to conquer and overcome the disability of radiations which he carries. There is one great control of these radiations. You are born under certain stars and it is those stars which control the flow of rays or radiation, the flow of spiritual light and the flow of material light or darkness. Therefore, it is important that you should know as soon as you begin to study spiritual things exactly where you stand in the physical, etheric and soul-bodies in the world of men today. Do you attract Light or Darkness? Did you come to Earth to give more Light or to attract Darkness that you may show yourself strong enough to control it? That is the only reason man touches Darkness on the Earth-plane, that he may be strong enough completely to control and overcome it.

In addition to the radiation of your own body, as you develop you become more and more subject to the rays or radiations from other people. If you have prepared yourself rightly in the Silence, in the understanding of the power of the aura, in the guiding and the purpose of the etheric body which acts as a filter both for the spiritual bodies and for the physical, you will realise that your etheric body must be kept as clean and as pure as your outward appearance. You would not go about the world with a dirty face or unwashed hands, but how often the face and the hands appear dirty to the highly trained spiritual psychic simply because the radiations of the etheric body have not been cleansed in prayer or through the silence in meditation, or have not been cared for by the understanding of the work of the chakra within these bodies of Light.

II

Very few people, either students of spiritual philosophy or ordinary men and women, realise the enormous importance of the invisible rays which permeate our physical bodies, our etheric bodies and our astral bodies, and link us with the great forces of God.

These include not only the mighty rays of light which emanate from the Godhead, but also those rays which pass through the Hierarchy of Angels, the great Muster of Masters and the lesser Muster of Teachers down through the more ordinary workers who come from the world of Spirit very close to the Earth to guide and direct mankind.

Modern man decries Astrology unless he is one of those students who have already learned the value of it, but we cannot ignore the fact that our birth is not accidental and that we come to Earth at a moment which links us with certain stars and planets in the heavens.

The planets are other worlds like our Earth, but having a different function in the etheric space. Each planet has its own quarter of the Earth to direct and in a sense govern. It is responsible for giving certain rays through certain stars and constellations to the Earth itself.

The Moon has a particular function in that it is responsible for the cultivation of the Earth. All growing things respond to the vibration of the Moon; also the tides respond. When there is great drought upon the Earth the Moon's function is more or less withdrawn because without water the vibrations of the Moon are useless – that is, they do not fit together. The vibrations of the Moon and the vibrations of the Earth during famine act in a warlike manner on each other and destroy each other. When you are born under a given planet, you are not alone in the acceptance of the rays of that planet. Hundreds and thousands of other souls are also responsible for accepting the rays, and these rays must be passed through myriads of stars before they are in a fit condition to touch the physical body of man. They must also pass through his soul-body, influencing his brain and mind, and they must accept the charge of the physical body, expecting the physical body to respond to them and to apply the right diet and remedies which are suitable for keeping the body in tune with them.

That is one of the points in which modern medicine fails, because it applies drugs and various drug injections which cure disease for the time being but do not go deeply enough into the source of the disease, nor do they cleanse or build the body. The modern doctor is apt to forget that before his remedies can take effect the body must be cleansed, and that after the remedies have been applied the body must be rebuilt, because as you put foreign bodies into your body the whole body is influenced and frequently changed; therefore remedies must be applied which will bring the body back to normal as nearly as possible.

Every soul born into the physical body brings his own ray, which is a gift of God. Some of these rays are gold, others are silver, others are coloured – as many colours as you can consider, so that the soul starts off from the Place of Light enveloped in his own colour. That colour enfolds his etheric body until the etheric body is practically entirely the ray-power and colour; it is thus that it enters the physical body.

There are children who are born mentally deficient because the soul refuses to accept at the moment of incarnation the life to which he is coming; that is because the soul – during those last passages before birth – must review the life which he has chosen and planned under the guidance of God, to fulfil in the physical body in this particular incarnation. When the soul rejects the incarnation, being fearful and afraid and not feeling strong enough, not having enough faith to accept under the guidance of God, the ray withdraws very slightly. Because of that withdrawal of the ray, the Light is withdrawn and the soul does not fully incarnate.

Some souls are incarnate more closely than others and therefore are permitted to carry a portion of the ray. These souls are teachable on certain lines with certain understanding. The majority of these souls that withdraw must remain outside the physical body, outside the personality, during the period of incarnation in physical life. They must make the long journey round the cycle of life again, not rejoining their component parts until after crossing the Bridge of Death, for the physical body must die first before the full power of the ray he has rejected is manifested within it.

In addition to the ray which is your own ray, you will need during life, certain other rays. You will need rays which will direct your intellect, your mental capacity; you will need rays which will pour the right Light through your body for you to use your hands creatively, and you will need other rays to link your creative faculty with your mind, which is the organ of the soul. The children who will be born now and for many years to come will find it increasingly difficult to learn mentally unless they can also at the same time have sufficient occupation for their hands. You will find fidgettiness in the child who is passing through the transition stage when the Piscean rays are being withdrawn and the Aquarian rays are being poured forth. The Aquarian rays are of considerable strength and they are based almost entirely at the moment in the bloodstream.

Some of the highly evolved spiritual men and women whom you are touching in your world today have come with the full force of these rays, ready to open and show themselves at the given moment. Others must still work hard in order to combine their own ray with the power of the rays of others; that is to say, their ray is not entirely complete – they must link mentally, spiritually and very often physically, in order to bring the full power of their own ray into action. You will find many people who will not touch philosophical questions or seek to enquire into the basis of spiritual knowledge. They have not yet made the contact which will secure that completeness.

You are passing through a period of making important contacts. They may be just important personal contacts to you; they may have a later and greater bearing on your own life, or they may slip away so that we may not be able to bring you in touch with each other at all. But never lose the opportunity of a contact; never pass someone's smile without a smile of your own, for these contacts are people who have something to give you and you have something to give them.

When you sit in the silence, you will frequently be conscious of colour. You will be conscious also of certain emanations of colour which come to you when you close your eyes just before you go to sleep, and similarly before you wake. You will be conscious when you enter certain buildings of certain etheric colours on the ether. All these are rays of different kinds and conditions which you must touch, for every individual is like the sparrow described in the Bible. It is just as important that you should reach and touch the rays of Light which lead you on in your own spiritual work, as it is that the Queen should be given an opportunity of reaching out to the rays of Light which have been prepared for her protection on her many hazardous journeys.

How can you be conscious of these rays? How can you feel them when you cannot see them? That question comes to us so often. You can see them when you have learned to sit in the Silence, when you have come to value the power of the Spirit, when you have accepted at the hands of God some task for God which no one else can do. Then that planet, that star, which holds the power over your ordinary life and death, opens its doors and sends forth the mighty power of the ray which directs your own road. These rays are mighty; sometimes they are overwhelming, these rays that protect you from danger, but they must have an anchorage. Unless you prepare yourself to hold and keep the rays, we cannot do anything about it, for although we direct the rays towards you, they do not link in with the rays which are already within your body.

Those of you who are accustomed to sit in the Silence to fulfil your path in development will be conscious also of certain changes from time to time in your etheric body and in your aura. This again is a very important point, because at the moment when we fuse two or more rays there is always a spark and then complete fusion of the rays together, which is shown in the aura as Light and colour.

When you see the aura you see it as a radiant emanation from the physical body. The aura is a radiation or an extension of the physical body, but it is also more important than that because the aura is composed of the rays within your body. These rays are the rays of your planetary influence, passed down through myriads of stars, accepting from each star a little Light and giving in return a little Light also. They are then poured through your body which is prepared by those who guide you. The body is exactly ready to receive them. For there must be no cessation of your work. We cannot pass these rays to you in sleep unless your sleep is peaceful and strong, and much of your dreaming rests upon the power of the rays which are directed through your astral and etheric bodies during the hours of sleep. Much of your difficulty in what you call recollecting your dreams in the early morning is due to the acceptance of rays of different colours and texture.

During the day you live busy lives and yet during the day we must purify your physical body in order that it is able and ready to receive the rays. Every one of you has a ray of colour and Light to give to every one whom you meet and in return that soul is called upon to give you his contribution. In some cases it would appear almost negligible but, like mercury, it can be divided and divided again until it is nothing but a pinpoint of silver light.

12.　*The Spiral of Life*

We are going to touch the spirals of life and the way they affect
your lives today and bring you in touch with those incidents of the
past which you are called upon to fulfil in this day of time. We
know of the work of Pythagoras and of the absolute necessity for
all who touch the teaching of Pythagoras to observe his rules,
which were strict, of many kinds, and touching many angles of
thought and service. A follower of Pythagoras must understand the
meaning of Truth, Integrity and Service. He must realise that
coming into a physical body is not only his own evolution but is to
assist in the evolution of all whom he touches. Many who are
craftsmen or who are guiding craftsmen today, have worked and
served under Pythagoras in the past and they will know well in their
own hearts how impossible it is for them to complete a task
imperfectly, or to allow another to complete his task without
perfection also.

The keynote of the work of Pythagoras is attention to detail.
That attention to detail is carried out entirely in material life, in
mental unfoldment and development, in spiritual unfoldment and
development, and in craftsmanship. Those who are craftsmen are
called upon to develop unusually strongly the psychic gifts with
which many thousands of men and women today are endowed.

Among those men and women are many who do not know or
understand the meaning of the psychic-spiritual development, but

we know and we understand. And we know, too, that our own gifts of the spirit can only unfold and develop if we are prepared to follow the path of Truth, Integrity and Service. You may think that truth and integrity are one and the same thing, but they are not entirely. Integrity has a wider meaning and draws within its auspices all gifts and service which are called upon to take their place in the life of man.

We are reaching the moment on this great cycle of evolution when the great fight between Darkness and Light is imminent. Never has there been a greater ugliness of darkness or a greater beauty of light, and therefore when beauty and light come together with darkness they are evenly matched. All that we need is the larger number of followers on one side to gain the victory, and we work for the victory of Light over Darkness.

That is why we pray, that is why we withdraw into quiet places to indulge in meditation and concentration. That is why we go forth in service, seeing among the people of the world children who are being built for the New Age of Aquarius, who will bring to the heart of man the gladness of light, the joy of truth and simplicity, which man today lacks. Those children are being prepared by the world of spirit to take their places on the sides of light and Right. At the same time, we see throughout the world a great darkness of shame, of selfishness and self-centredness, of jealousy and resentment, of darkness, overshadowing evil in the hearts of men who seek to harm their brothers, great cruelty, great disension and in many ways great horror on the part of those who follow the path of Darkness.

What is this Spiral of Life? Your soul comes into incarnation upon a spiral. As you leave the Place of Light you move gently but surely round that spiral, incarnating and dying in each place of consciousness through which you pass, leaving something of yourself behind, taking something of the plane itself with you, until you come to earth to be born in the physical body of a man. You may hesitate at the moment of birth, for you must review the life to which you are coming.

The Spiral of Life

It is a life which has been planned by you with those who guide you, with the Masters of Wisdom under whom you are going to serve and under the guidance of the Father-Mother God Himself. You pass through physical life in the material body of flesh, drawing power and sustenance through your soul from the Place of Light, and touching in sleep, as you progress, those Planes of Consciousness through which you have passed on your way to Earth. In those hours of sleep, the knowledge that you gain in life is expanded and developed upon those faraway Planes of Consciousness, and you return refreshed or unrefreshed according to your method of carrying the knowledge and the strength you have gained, and your ability to bring back a greater nourishment for the day's work and service.

All the time you are moving in circles, surrounding the spiral of life, coming and going, moving slowly and swiftly, according to the way which God has designed for you. Every day during your physical life you make fresh contacts. You may make a contact with Nature or with one of God's creatures. You may make a contact with a man or a woman whom you have known before, or someone you have never met before. You may pass close, upon a pathway of this great city, to someone who can give you very much more than anyone else can give you at that particular moment in your life. Therefore it is important that, in all you do and say and think, you should dwell in harmony of thought, in love to all men, to all creatures and to all life.

If you are on a spiral of Pythagoras, he who is the Great Master of the New Age, you will touch morality, science and religion from entirely new angles. If you have advanced mentally in this new teaching, you will be able to grasp and to hold the teaching that Pythagoras will give you. You will carry that teaching with you through the hours of sleep and through the waking day, until it becomes part of your very life. Although the life in the physical body seems long, it is but a short span compared to the time you are to spend out of the physical body, in the etheric places through which you will be called to work and serve.

The Spiral of Life

The basis of the teaching of the Aquarian Age is the separation of morality from religion. We shall find that the new morality will have no function with religion. In religion, we worship God, we serve Him according to His law – and the new Tables of the Law for the life of the Aquarian Christ are being prepared. From time to time a student will be given a vision of these Tables, on which are written in symbols of gold the teaching of the New Age in Morality, Science and Religion. But before you can touch this teaching, you must learn the power of the Darkness and the necessity that this Darkness should work itself out, and not be carried forward by those who serve God under the guidance of the Master Pythagoras.

We see a world which to us appears immoral and cruel, and the immorality and the cruelty of the world must reach its zenith before the Sword of Michael can strike. Where the sword cleaves, Light shall follow, and in the cleft of the sword we shall find the Light expanding, dividing the Darkness into two parts. Where Darkness is divided by Light it cannot stand. That Light will be Truth – absolute, complete and perfect Truth.

Where the sword cleaves, you will see a new morality come forth. A morality which will bring Light and happiness to the new world which prepares for the Way of the Aquarian Christ, and the cruelty and the darkness will flee away and the glory of the Light of God will remain. Out of the dark science of war and turmoil and tumult, the building of force and the preparation of instruments of war, will come flames of fire. Through that fire shall the sword of Pythagoras again cleave, and the fire will become no longer the consuming fire of darkness, but the cleansing fire of God, which is symbolised for you each year in the Whitsun Festival, the festival of the Purification by Fire.

Man shall learn to handle the weapons of science with knowledge, and that knowledge shall include the Way of God. For it will be a very long time before the men who use science, and all that it means, shall bow their heads to God, for God must bring to them the knowledge that He is God, not a Being created from the fantasy of man, but a Living God of Love. When man has had enough of scientific warfare and destruction, he will reach out with both hands for the Love of God and hold it for evermore.

And religion! We feel very sad when we examine the religions of the world today; the graft and self-seeking, self-interest, the darkness of subterfuge and pretence, all must come to a climax. Out of that climax shall grow a new Faith which will see God as He is, and open the eyes of men to see Him and know Him and love Him.

All these things were prepared for the children of men by Pythagoras himself. He, it was, who brought the glory of the light to the Oracle of Delphi, who established the Pythoness to guide men nearer to God, by the Word of God poured through her mouth to the children of men. He, it was, who brought, through attention to minute detail, the glory of the drawn figure, the carven stone, the measured instrument of complete perfection − all that it meant to man to build his own temple, and in that temple to find the Living God.

He lives anew in the hearts of men today, for out of the darkness he brings light, he strengthens the divination of the seer, he teaches men how to see with the eyes of the spirit, to hear with the ears of the spirit, and to accentuate the power of the spirit through other senses yet unknown to man. But in all things, Pythagoras works for perfection, and therefore we who serve him are called to serve him with perfection on all planes of consciousness. We may not achieve that perfection in this life but the nearer we grow to it, the stronger we belong to it and the closer we are to God.

You meet much darkness in the world. You meet men who are cruel and hard, who have a complete lack of understanding of the things which are dear to you. But that knowledge which is given to you can be put forth by you as power, and power is kindness, and kindness is extended to friendship. And power and kindness and friendship are love, which is the basis of life.

There is a very great difference between being kind and solicitous for your friend, and being interfering and dominant. The dominant spirit must go because it holds the darkness of the self and encourages those who use it to be self-seeking, self-interested and self-attributive.

When you kneel in a Sanctuary remember this: that the path of God calls you, and on that path the three major lessons which you must learn — morality, science and religion — are waiting for you to touch the locks which will open the door to each one of you in turn. Each of these attributes of God contains and possesses the Glory of God. And you can reach them.

You may think that, because you were born in a part of the world which knows nothing of seership, you have no power to see or to hear the voice of spirit, to hear the sounds of music in the etheric planes, but you have that power. For the moment you open your heart to God, He will speak to you; the moment you unfold your spirit and lay it before Him, you will hear Him. And once you have heard Him you will never forget His voice, and you will never cease to do His service under His own guiding hand.

But fulfil your material task first. For when Pythagoras built his Temple of Learning, and measured the stones of the foundation so that there was no joint missing, no space, no badness of placing, no misunderstanding of quality, he chose the best and he placed the best.

Look at the work of science today. Realise the calculation, and the attention to detail, which has gone to the erection of these immense buildings, the depth of the foundations, for which have been chosen the best that man could find in workmen and tools and material. Watch the work of the scientist as it grows. Scientific man, by building these great edifices, is seeking to reach God in the only way he knows, by climbing a spiral staircase in an edifice of bricks and wood and stone.

The seer climbs to God a different way. He withdraws into the silence and thanks God for His Glory and the beauty of life, and he sets himself apart in prayer and worship and self-sacrfice. He does not reach the heights in such a spectacular way as the scientist but he gets there all the same, and it is he who will help the religious side to manifest also. For then the churchman realises and accepts the fact that God alone can heal the sick, whether He heals them through the hands of a healer, or the mind of a psychologist, or the drugs of a doctor. The healer, the psychologist and the doctor must all have a little of each other to give the patient, to make him whole, and when he is whole the triangle is perfect and the Light can flow.

13.   *The Origin of the Bloodstream*

We need to link up one or two points on Radiesthesia in connection with the bloodstream. There are many hundreds of people today who are concerned with the scientific side of these matters but leave out the spiritual side altogether.

The Scientist must at all times turn his thought to accepting spiritual things as well as scientific things, and to join them together. He will not join them together too soon, and he will watch the two currents side by side. He will work things upon the positions of the scientific facts which he needs for his diagnosis, and he will at the same time be conscious of the spiritual power around him, which guides him. Therefore he has the right to say: 'I am an intuitional thinker'.

Machines are being used for the diagnosis of the bloodstream and are being brought to perfection. Those who work upon them leave their spiritual ideas, their spiritual thoughts and their spiritual communications outside the workshop, but from time to time they are called upon to put two points together in a new way. Then they realise that, at the back of their minds, there is the knowledge as to how they can put those two points together. They are able to assemble the points and to make a new idea, which will later be carried out in a formula and the formula put into practical use.

Within the physical bloodstream of man lies the cosmic

111

bloodstream which plays an important part in healing, now and in the future.

We believe in the reincarnation of the soul. We know that the soul contains, or is made up of, spiritual organs which link him to God. We know that the mind of the soul is directly in contact with the mind of God, when the soul is guiding the personality upon the path of life in the right way.

When the first, compulsory incarnations are completed, the soul stands to give account of itself – in a sense, to speak to our Father-Mother God and tell him what the result of these compulsory incarnations have been. Every soul incarnating for the first time has certain lessons to learn during the first life. They are very simple lessons, they are lessons of obedience to the will of man and to the will of God, they are lessons of unselfishness and of placing God first. That is all that God asks of the young soul. Therefore, when the young soul at the end of his compulsory incarnations stands before the face of God, the sheet of parchment giving the account of his lives will show distinctly how far he has gone in the fulfilment of these particular tasks.

He will have had certain difficulties, for all young souls go into incarnation with the same difficulties and setbacks – they are not like the older souls who come voluntarily into incarnation, accepting a way of life which must be governed by the soul they have learned to respect and to love. Therefore the soul, which in most of you is visible in Light but is an invisible radiance, stands before the Father-Mother God and by the rays that he emits he answers the questions upon the parchment which our Father-Mother God uses to verify the facts of the soul. Then he goes away for a while and he learns certain lessons in the Place of Light, but they will not touch the faults and failings that he has presented at his reception. He will see the lives of other people working out in Light in the seventh plane of the Astral. For a long period of time the soul will remain in the seventh plane of the Astral, watching other souls and the work they are doing as a result of their compulsory incarnations, realising where he could have done better and realising also that he was given a very great deal of Power which he has wasted. Once he realises that, the soul is ready to become very humble, and it is at the moment of humility that he is called by the Lords of Karma to decide whether he wants to reincarnate into an earthly body again or whether he wants to remain without further advancement on the seventh plane.

The plan, we will suppose, is decided, that the soul will return to the Earth, is given an opportunity of choosing his parents and these parents' lives have already been planned and arranged. Shall we suppose that at the moment when he first meets them in the Spirit they are ready to incarnate into the physical body, and a certain radiance from them enters his own soul in the etheric, and certain light, power, knowledge and understanding, go from him to his parents-to-be. They reincarnate and during the period that they are descending from the Place of Light to the Earth-plane to be born as infants in the world of men, a very great preparation has to be made by the soul that is going to become their child. He will be taken in the etheric over and over again by the Beings who are called upon to be his Guides, to the Earth, to watch them incarnate, to watch them grow from infancy to childhood, from childhood to adolescence, from adolescence to the full adult life, until the moment comes when they are ready and joined in the ceremony which is called marriage upon the Earth-plane. Then the child must be ready to begin his journey to the Earth.

It is only when the first light passes from the coming child to the parents, at the moment of conception, that the child in the etheric planes is called upon to consider the make-up of his body. The most important part of that make-up is the gift of God which is the Cosmic bloodstream, which is Light, which is Love.

To the soul awaiting preparation, this golden stream is a great joy. It is warm, full of radiance and full of promise. It gives him the feeling that he is coming down to a new life, to be loved and cared for, to be educated and brought up, and to be given an opportunity to show the love of God in the world to which he is going. All through that period of descent, the cosmic bloodstream within the

113

radiance of the etheric body is being moulded and prepared to the image of God within the coming child.

It is not for a long time that the soul can do anything more than cherish the cosmic bloodstream within itself, because the radiance of the soul held by the Light of the etheric planes through which it is passing on its journey to Earth holds all that is good: Spirit, Love, Joy. The soul feels that round itself is being moulded a structure which will act as a protection for himself, his very soul, and which will give him an opportunity of expressing all the organs of the physical body in Light, because of the Light that he carries as the great main bloodstream of all.

When, in its descent, the soul reaches the seventh plane of the Astral, all the vibrations of nature are conjoined and added to it. It must pass through the Garden of Remembrance, seeking the trees and the plants, and the people that it knows, and draw from each a gift. That gift is something, and the giving is something, which can only be described as an incredible radiance. For every soul that makes a gift to a soul journeying to the Earth brings the radiance of the cosmic bloodstream towards him, and out of that cosmic bloodstream are manufactured, or drawn, tiny fragments which form the corpuscles of the physical bloodstream.

How very often the psychic researchers say: 'Why aren't we told the origin of the bloodstream?' It is because without the spiritual knowledge that lies behind it they could not possibly understand the make-up.

The gifts that are made in the seventh plane of the Astral, from the souls that love the incoming soul and want to wish him well on his journey, all become part of that last etheric sheath which is the last covering on the entrance to the Earth and the first covering of the infant. If you look at an infant or a growing child up to the age of about a year, you will see a radiance of moving Light like a bubble of light, violet and blue, green and mauve and white, and in that radiance, the golden light of the bloodstream itself. The bloodstream alone flows through and governs every organ of the body, every part of the body. Without the bloodstream the muscles

114

and the bones cannot grow. Without the bloodstream the heart cannot beat, and without the beat of the heart, the golden part of God which is within every incarnate human being cannot open to accept the love of God.

There are human beings who seem to have no love of God within them, no feeling for their fellow-men, no desire to become one with nature in order to make their way to becoming one with God. But the bloodstream, the physical bloodstream, cannot exist without the light of the cosmic bloodstream, and although the Light of the cosmic bloodstream depends entirely upon the previous life of the soul and what it has brought into the world as its gift to the world, it nevertheless commands and discovers every drop of blood which is in the body of the incarnate soul.

If we watch the men who are working so incredibly hard and under so much divine guidance in making these radionic instruments, we shall realise that they are touching the physical bloodstream only, and therefore they are not really touching the mind of the patient whose blood they are treating. They are touching the mind of the patient by the power of thought, and that is a very different matter. They cannot touch the mind of the soul, which is the mind of God, and learn God's will for the soul that they are treating, unless they are able to read the mind of God within the bloodstream which is the cosmic stream of golden Light itself.

When we talk more closely to men who are giving their whole lives to scientific investigation of these matters, we are conscious that they know there is something which is eluding them. They can draw from the bloodstream information which will guide them in their diagnosis, they can draw from that selfsame bloodstream the condition of sickness which they want to treat, but as yet at no time can they treat the mind of the soul, which is the mind of God.

You say: 'Is it permitted to treat the mind of God?' What we are endeavouring to bring to the knowledge of spiritual and scientific researchers ourselves, is the fact that without prayer, without the knowledge of the golden Light of God, without the Power of the

115

love of God, the bloodstream will not speak to them. And until, on their instruments, they can persuade the bloodstream to speak to them, they cannot achieve the complete knitting together of the personality and the soul.

That is the whole cure of disease. Disease is disharmony: dis-ease, dis-harmony. The rhythms which are within the physical body are jarring against the rhythms within the soul. The Light within the soul is endeavouring to strengthen the physical body but cannot do so unless there is complete harmony between soul and body. Place your feet upon the path you have chosen under the guidance of God to tread. Seek the harmony which lies between soul and body, not in yourself but in others, and give with full hearts all that you have of knowledge, of power, of love. Bring to light all that the bloodstream holds, all that it uses in the service of men and of God in the strengthening and the building up of the organs of the body. For without the building up of the bloodstream, and the harmony that it needs for that up-building, man cannot be whole.

That is why you are seeing so much apparent Darkness. All this rebellion among the young people, all these difficulties which surround you. People are unhappy and discontented because they are not touching the things of the Spirit, to bring them into harmony with the things of the soul. One day all that will clear away, for the disharmony must appear in order that the Light may be closed in and protected while disharmony surrounds them. When the disharmony is cleansed and purified, harmony returns, until it fills the world of men with the knowledge and love of God, with the gratitude for all he has created in all living things, the life blood of God given within, the life blood of nature, of man, of plant, of all that God has created. Even the mud which fouls your feet as you walk upon it, contains in some small measure the spark of life which you need to join to your own bloodstream for this up-building. So despise not the little happenings and remember that all that disciplines your physical life radiates life into your bloodstream, and from within your bloodstream into the body and so through to the soul.

116

14. *The Magnetic Force*

You come to earth upon a spiral of evolution. You work round in a cycle to the moment when you began the cycle, and then you go forward on a higher spiral, again through another circle or cycle of life. That has been going on every time you came to earth, but each time you have been incarnate you have come down through just one plane of consciousness and then another to the earth life. Perhaps coming through those planes of consciousness you have remembered little incidents of a previous coming, and you need to learn to classify those incidents and to realise the bearing they have on your life today.

When you are born into the earth you have already completed one cycle through coming down to earth, and then you are set upon another road to complete a cycle of evolution in the body. When that cycle is entirely completed, you cross the Bridge of Death to return to the place from which you came, to the same planes of consciousness, but with a very different outlook, because you carry a certain amount of the earth memory forward with you. Therefore, whereas when you come to earth your consciousness is tinged with the Light of God, when you leave the earth to return to God your consciousness is tinged, and very often overcome, with the incidents of the earthly life.

During your earth life you move round in certain cycles of evolution, and each time you reach the end of a cycle you are moving a slightly greater step forward on the path. The experiences that you have taken in that one cycle of life are expressed when you

117

reach the end of the cycle, and if you have taken those experiences well, you move forward on a little higher reach of the path. If you have taken them badly, you go back round the cycle. Because you have not enough impetus or power to raise yourself on the cycle, if you have completed the cycle in darkness or dimness or in an unsatisfactory manner.

When a group of people are studying the things of the spirit we must endeavour to keep them on the same level of study and consciousness. If there are one or two who fail to complete their cycle and must remain behind, it is very difficult indeed for the others to catch up or to wait for them to come along. They should endeavour to keep even: there should not be any who go too far ahead, there should not be any who lag behind — they should complete the cycles together, synchronised in perfect harmony. To do that we must come to an understanding within ourselves of the meaning and the power of vibration, for vibration plays a very important part in our lives today.

When man leaves the place of light, as a rule there are two paths marked for him. These paths are different and alternative, and they can run together as one path quite a long way in life and then be separated. As an instance of this, there were two paths which were marked for Christ Jesus. When Jesus, the Great Master, was chosen to fulfil that path of life on earth which he did fulfil in all its entirety, He also had to wait until all things were ready for His Coming.

You, before you came to earth, chose your parents. If your parents came together in marriage early in life, your path was the first path which has been marked for you, because through being born of them you were definitely exactly on the point which you were meant to take. That point may have happened early, but if your parents met late in life, through some accident which was not foreseen and which could not be avoided by either parent, then you came to earth later in life, and because the configuration of the planets and the stars was slightly different, you would find a quite different path had been accepted by your soul.

The Master Jesus was directly descended from David, the King, because His earthly father, Joseph, was a reincarnation of King David. That is to say, the soul of Joseph was the soul of King David. And the path that was marked for the Master Jesus to take, if He had to take it with all the suffering and the sorrow that it entailed, was definitely as the son of Joseph and Mary, Joseph being the reincarnation of King David, and Mary, the Mother, a reincarnation of Miriam, thus linking the Master Jesus with Moses. But because the earth conditions had not been exactly right at the moment when He was due to come, and through coming to birth in life He would have touched a path which was not really His, He was held back, and He came to earth on that secondary path, the path of sorrow and of suffering. If He had come as was ordained, He should have come as the Pharaoh Santananda. he would have incarnated in Egypt instead of in Israel, and He would have been a great earthly King, not a spiritual King as He eventually became.

It is not for us to consider which was the better path, but we must realise that when a Leader incarnates on a given path, all those whose lives are planned to surround that leader are brought into incarnation at the same moment and for the same purpose. Therefore if we put out of our minds the fact that Menalik, who eventually incarnated as the Pharaoh Santananda, was the son of Solomon, we shall remember that either way Jesus could have incarnated as the son of David. Therefore, the beginning of the path was made right, and because all men are born in the image of Christ Jesus and hold the Power of Christ Jesus in such proportion as they have earned it, all men must follow that selfsame path. Therefore, we find throughout the ages, in that great cycle of two thousand years, that the world has had to undergo suffering and to pass through great darkness, to reach a point of crisis before the Coming of a New Christ.

What could man do to bring back the Light to the world, that peace might come instead of war? He could join himself together in groups for prayer and meditation. He could prepare his own plan of life under the God-given word of Jesus. He could go forward under the very guidance of Jesus himself, working always for peace, but realising that that peace could only be obtained when

119

the world had passed through the purification of suffering.

You are finding, at the moment, strange understanding of the young about marriage. That is probably caused, although not in every case, by the fact that certain souls who have chosen those particular parents must come into incarnation at a given moment, but there is nothing to hold those parents together once the child is born and his feet set upon the path of earth. Only where real true love exists, can the marriage bond be reverenced and held true and clear to the end.

These are the things of the Spirit and we must prepare our thoughts for the understanding that there are still a large number of souls who should be incarnate at this moment and who have a part to play in the peace of the world, bringing peace to the world. Therefore we must face this event in life with the understanding of the spirit.

If you go carefully into a study of the time of the birth of Christ Jesus, you will find there is an extraordinary misunderstanding among theologians and other scientific people about the moment and period of the Birth. You will base your understanding of the moment of Birth upon the fact that there was a configuration of Saturn and Jupiter, two important planets of the Piscean Age in the year 6 B.C., and it was the vibration and the power from those planets which caused the birth of Christ Jesus to happen when it did. It took six years for the power of that configuration to impregnate the earth, to prepare the earth that it should be a fit place for the Child to be born, otherwise the Light would not have been ready in such a way that it could be given to all men.

It is essential for each one to build a firm foundation. The foundation is a rock or a stone. The Master Jesus spoke to Peter saying: 'Thou art Peter; upon this Rock will I build My Church'. Of course, Christ Jesus could only build His Church if the earth upon which Peter and the other disciples stood was ready for the building.

Therefore, it was the power from Saturn and Jupiter which filled the earth, which penetrated the earth, which went deep down into the soil of Israel, and through the vibration which returned to it. All things that are projected from God are returned to God, whether of good or evil. The projection of the magnetic force from the earth back to God made it possible to set in motion the great space-ship which held that tremendous force of light, of fire, of glory, which appeared to the Shepherds and which, moving across the sky, led the Wise Men from the East to the manger bed. The only people who saw that Star were those whose hearts and minds were ready for the Light, who had been drawn in to that magnetic force from the earth projected from Saturn to Jupiter, and were held in the Light.

In the Bible we are told how the Angel said to the Shepherds: 'Arise, go find the young Child', how the voice spoke to the Wise Men: 'A Child is born'. Those who had worked with them realised that that Child had been born upon the very moment calculated for His birth, and when they set out on their long weary journey they were guided by the Star. Neither the Shepherds nor the Wise Men could have been even conscious, because when they were guided it was not only by their own eyes. They were guided by that magnetic force which made them go forward, just as you feel sometimes you cannot rest until you have undertaken and completed some small and apparently trivial task. It is because you are within a certain circle, or cycle of vibration, which makes it essential that you should complete that task at the moment that you know within yourself it must be completed.

Both the Shepherds and the Wise Men were reincarnated. They had dwelt in Atlantis, where space-ships were known and used as easily as you use your aeroplanes. Your aeroplanes are a different shape. Space-ships are much more flat. The aeroplane has lights, and everyone who sees those lights knows that the lights are artificial. But those with the eyes of the Spirit can see the guiding light round the aeroplane. When an aeroplane sets forth in a vibration to which it does not belong, which is not tuned-in to the earth's magnetic field, for which it has not been prepared on the journey, it will have a totally different significance in the sky from the aeroplane whose journey has been prepared by being put within that magnetic field and force, and held there from the beginning of its journey to the end.

Each one must understand the importance of preparing their own light. It is your light which builds your foundation. It is your light which brings peace into your own soul which you can give out to others. It is your knowledge which is light, which is truth, which can help others to build their own foundations. You are working, not only with the thoughts of the spirit and the power of the spirit, but you are working within vast magnetic fields. If space-ships come you may not be conscious of their presence, but it was both humble and great men who saw the Star in the East, which was the space-ship of the past and will be the space-ship which will herald the Coming of the New Christ, the Christ of Aquarius.

Every incident in the life of Christ Jesus will be carried out in the life of the Aquarian Christ, but it will go the other way round. As Jesus completed His life from babyhood to middle-age, the New Christ will come to earth a fully grown man, a Being of Light, carrying Light and brought by Light, and He will work back the other way. So that from the great esoteric knowledge which He will bring, He will work back through the hearts of the men of the world until He touches the simplicity of the little child, as Jesus foretold would happen.

Though you work from childhood to old age, you will come to a point, when you will know what it means to grow from old age to youth, and to enjoy every moment of it. Because you will have learned to build your foundation, and to draw towards your foundation that magnetic force without which you cannot progress in the world of Spirit. The magnetic force which attaches you to the earth is the great force which God gives to mankind for the healing of his body, the healing of his mind, the healing of his heart.

There are some who are more close to the soil than others, and those must return to the soil every time they falter or fail upon the earth path. Because only through the soil can they make contact with that great magnetic field, the same magnetic field which was used to destroy the Walls of Jericho.

122

15. *Radiation of the Light*

From time to time we need to return to our understanding of the conditions of incarnation during the Atlantean period. It is important that we should understand these conditions in order to see how the whole cycle of life from the beginning of time has evolved to return to the Godhead.

We will leave the etheric Temple itself out of the picture and touch that part of the history of Atlantis when souls were incarnate in the physical body for the purpose of the reproduction of the race for the first time as infants. Until that time, which was linked with the people of the Valley, the soul had come to earth fully-grown and able to take its own way, but once the incarnation in the flesh became part of the plan of life, we find souls incarnating under the Divine Plan according to place and climate and country, so that they came into certain groups of people who surrounded the great Atlantean Hill in large numbers. Imagine the valley being divided into sections, and souls being drawn into incarnation in these different sections.

This method of incarnation continued until the Mystery of Golgatha, or almost until that moment. Every change of era is marked by the fulfilment of a mystery.

The Mysteries which form initiations are small. They concern small groups of people attached to certain Temples or certain buildings. But the great Mysteries which affect the whole of mankind are of the greatest possible importance in the understanding of spiritual change. The Mystery of Golgatha began with the birth of Christ and ushered in a new age of new laws, new understanding, new outlook. The Mystery which is being prepared for the fulfilment of the coming of the New Christ is one in which the spirit must raise its consciousness to the highest possible level, remembering that it has had to descend into matter in order to learn to raise that consciousness.

So that, where the first period of incarnation which was regulated by place and natural conditions was the descent of spirit into matter, man has now evolved sufficiently to return to spirit by raising his consciousness, through his experiences in matter, to the consciousness of the Godhead.

So we see man coming to the point which was reached at the birth of Jesus, when a steady stream of people was beginning to move around all over the world. This was because the impulse of incarnation was no longer part of place and the natural surroundings of people. The souls that had returned to the place of Light up to that moment were no longer called upon to incarnate just to live the life of earth, but in order to evolve their own souls by further contact with material conditions. It is at this moment that we find material conditions into which the soul should incarnate, planned, in order to achieve the development of the soul. This particular form of incarnation caused a tremendous movement of peoples, so that the peoples of the world began at that point to mix with other peoples. Until that moment they had been entirely separated.

If you study history from the birth of Christ you will find that enormous movements of people were to be seen. The Angles and the Saxons came forth from Europe to Britain and founded a new nation of people there. They had a greater culture, a greater civilisation, and they brought that culture and civilisation with them in order that they might radiate the light of that culture where they dwelt, in what was apparently a savage land. Through the radiation of that light further light could be built from the world of spirit to aid the incoming souls. To civilise an uncivilised people does not consist of a nation which is more mentally and spiritually advanced impressing itself upon that people. It means that the particular nation which possesses the culture radiates such light that that light penetrates the hearts of the so-called uncivilised peoples and lights the candle of the heart, which radiates that greater light of the spirit.

In history books we find a very great deal of importance attached to the Renaissance period, and the Renaissance was caused through the Turks advancing through Greece towards Italy. They drove the Greeks – who were a highly intellectual race, strong mentally, physically and spiritually, a highly evolved race – further West, and these Greeks brought their culture to the Western part of Europe through the light which they were able to radiate from within and to leave behind them wherever they moved.

Every thought, every movement, every word you utter, has an effect upon the ether. The senses, being the gateways of the soul as it were, pick up those radiations which you pour out. If they are good, then those radiations return through your senses as light. If they are evil or ugly, or only slightly dark, they return to you as darkness, or less light.

These radiations are the primary cause of disease in the physical body today. It is not only your own radiations; it is the radiations of others which you absorb. But you will not absorb the darkness through the radiations of other people if you yourself are able, through your senses, to radiate light, and it is that radiation of light which is the basis of Aquarian healing work. All healers must be able to radiate light through their five senses in order that that light may return as light through their own soul, and then, growing to a greater light, may be shed on all others. That is why the Aquarian healer is called to work upon the senses of his patient. If the senses radiate light, and are cleansed and purified with light, then the whole body is full of light.

There is a tendency today to consider the physical body, the metabolism, as the only thing that matters, and with that there comes the strange belief that it does not matter in the least what you absorb by way of the mouth into the physical body as it will always take care of itself. Now that is not so. Your physical body, the metabolism, which is the third aspect of the Trinity of bodies of which you are composed, must be in perfect wholeness in order that the light from within yourself may penetrate and the light from without may shine within.

You are living in an age of science, and this is a very important test, because science knows nothing of spirit. Scientific discovery is part and parcel of the age, and as man advances, unless he is very, very careful and has a great understanding of the things of the spirit, he will slowly and surely shut out spiritual things in preference for the scientific things.

Science, on the whole, makes its discoveries through the investigation of dead bodies. How can you study the living through the dead? You cannot do it. Where science touches the living, it is imbued with and enfolded by the spirit. But it is because of the advance of science, which needs dead bodies for its investigation, that you have so many wars and desire for atomic weapons, to create dead bodies, that the radiation from these bodies may be felt upon the ether and the investigations of the dead may continue.

There are two points which are of vital importance to modern man. He has been given the wholly glorious and wonderful gift of the spirit, and with that gift which lies within its own soul, he has been allowed to study and to know the mysteries of the spirit. This study of the mysteries unfolds and develops within him his own soul in radiations of light, and if that development is undertaken in the right way, and the life of the man is right and strong and true and he treads his own path rightly, then the radiations from the spirit within the soul will be strong enough to support any amount of scientific study. He will draw spirit from science. And at this very moment, when science and religion are brought so close to each other, they are beseeching from the world of spirit that the religious man will welcome science and try to understand it, and that the scientific man will welcome spiritual things and try to understand them.

Because it is a scientific age, an age of crisis which must be worked out upon the physical plane, you must go through that crisis to strengthen your spirit. Your spirit must be able to soar beyond the earth and all earthly things, and so raise its consciousness that it may completely be enfolded in the age of Aquarius in the etheric pattern of life, whereas now it is enfolded in the physical. That is why it is so important that every man and woman shall play their part in the world of men in this day of time. Because that part which has been given to you has been prepared specially for you, that you should do your little bit, that you should fill your little corner of the universe, with the perfection which God has given you.

No longer are you called to incarnate in a special race which depends upon mountains or valleys, or climatic conditions or natural surroundings. You are called upon to incarnate in the very middle of the world of men, where you will meet the minority of spiritual-thinking people. You will also meet an enormous amount of materialism – materialism crystallised and hardened into the heart of the materialist. Among all these you will meet a great many materialists who will have upon their lips a certain spiritual patter.

These people will seem shallow to you because you are of the spirit. They will say that life has been given to them to live, and they are going to live it and enjoy it to the full. And they live it, they become selfish and they forget God, if they ever acknowledged that God existed. In a sense they hurt you spiritually, because that patter of spiritual things means nothing at all. What you need is that deep strength of purpose which knows the right, and which is endeavouring with all the strength in its hands, in its heart, in its senses, to link together the three bodies of man: the physical, which is the metabolism upon which material man works, the spiritual body and the soul.

Your metabolism depends very largely for health and strength upon the way you use it spiritually. Your breath and the exercises in breathing which you do — in those you are linking with the breath of God, for it is the breath of God within you which holds together those three bodies. It is the breath which sets the rhythm of these bodies and that rhythm is picked up by the tiny drop of fluid in your spinal column. The metabolism of the body works according to the rhythm of the spinal fluid, which takes its rhythm from the breath. That rhythm is communicated through the spine and through the breath to the bloodstream.

If you have lived well and rightly, and you have drawn in through your own five senses that etheric light, you will find that that light will pour through the bloodstream, light up the cosmic bloodstream and radiate to without. But if you have shut down on the radiations which prepare the rhythm of your bodies, then there cannot be any distinctive rhythm and they will be at variance, and it is at those moments when you feel that your feet are off the path and you feel lost. It is based on rhythm; the rhythm of the spinal column which is communicated through the metabolism of the body by the bloodstream and accepted from the breath. The heart, the lungs, all the vital organs of the body depend upon this rhythm, and that is what the Aquarian healer is called upon to do in his healing work.

Where it is possible to repair the radiations in such a way that light may enter the physical body to strengthen the organs with light, he is called upon to adjust the mind of his patient, especially in the case of a child, so that the rhythm of the bodies may flow entirely through to the soul. Where it is an adult, he must show him exactly the point where the breath and the spine and the bloodstream are moving out of harmony and where his feet are off the path and he is feeling lost and in confusion.

There are certain laws which are known as the laws of God. I do not connect these laws so much with the laws of Moses. The laws that I want to call the laws of God are those laws which were brought to earth direct from God by the Master Jesus under the direction of the Father-Mother God. Those are the laws under which we are working today. Every man is called upon to fulfil a place in life. Every parent, and pair of parents, is called to set their child upon the path which will lead him to that place. Less and less is the child today to be coerced or forced into a path that is unsuitable. He must learn that only when he has set himself completely in harmony with the Divine law may he look outside and see where he is called upon to help his fellowmen. Because, if, at one moment, you are radiating· unsatisfactory or impure thoughts or actions or wishes, you cannot possibly expect to turn the radiations of those wishes into light when you come in touch with someone who needs guidance and understanding.

That is why psychology is given to man to help him at this juncture, because man must understand the effect his words and deeds and thoughts have upon his fellowman in the physical body, in order to understand the working of the mind and the reaction from the mind of another towards his own way of thinking. Therefore, it is necessary that you should begin your spiritual training with a very firm desire for service. Service to God through truth, and through the effort so to harmonise your three bodies – three important bodies – that you are able to move through life without taking from anyone else any light which should be theirs and theirs only.

If you, as healers, are approached by a patient, then you must look very deeply into that patient's heart. Find out where he has gone wrong in his reaction towards life, in his understanding of the meaning of life. Because that training is due to someone who is living in a wrong way, a way across the will of God, thereby drawing power for his negative action and preventing the will of God coming into operation. Until you can convince him where he has gone wrong in his attitude to life and his fellowman, you cannot possibly hope to supplant that wrong way of living with light and right.

We do not decry science or the scientist. These are given to us at this particular moment in the history of the world, in order that we should understand them. It is for us, who are so filled with the gifts of the spirit that we have enough and overflowing to give away, to approach the scientist, so that we can work side by side with him, each giving to the other. As we give him light, he will approach with a greater desire for light — and through that desire for light he will meet God. Then, through the illumination which God will give him direct, as a reward for all his studies and his work and his groping and his desire, he will receive the reward of the spirit which will make all things plain to him.

16.   *The Initiation of Faith*

The third Initiation, which is given the symbol of the White Swan, is also, above all, the Initiation of Faith under the trials and the difficulties of man's life in the world today.

Faith is extremely difficult to touch and to hold. There were certain people who set out upon a path of One-ness with God to make men free and equal in the sight of men and God, to cut away the chains which bind man to his fellow-man in service, and to prepare freedom of physical life, freedom of mental life and freedom of spiritual life. They believed in eating no meat because to destroy life was wrong; they believed in holding peace because to fight was wrong; and their gospel was a right gospel, a gospel of truth, peace and love.

But they went far away from that gospel, for there infiltrated among them a body of revolutionaries who desired to make men slaves rather than free. Under the guise of freedom they called into being a movement which has gone far from the peace which it prophesied.

Those who come from the world of spirit to guide mankind are conscious of two distinct groups of men and women in the world: those who are enthused with the desire to prove immortality and through that proof to prove the existence of God, and those who desire to decry God, to drag Him down, to prove His non-existence.

The Spiral of Life

Some years ago we should have found a very much larger number of Godless men and women, but now those who worship God, who believe in Him, who are ready to prove the immortality of the soul, are far greater than those who seek to prove that there is no God. Those who work with you from the world of spirit find it very difficult indeed to believe and understand your difficulties in accepting the existence of God, and therefore they are trying from every possible angle to bring the knowledge of God and His work for men into the world of materialism as it stands today. All who work in the great spiritual movements will tell you that the faith of those with whom they work is stronger and greater than it has ever been, that never at any time in the history of the world has the power of the spirit of God been so living and enduring a flame as it is at the present moment – and yet it is hard to see and hard to find.

Therefore, we must band ourselves together with a great power of spirit, to fulfil the work which God seeks to fulfil through the children of men. We may not all be called to be leaders; we may not – many of us – be called to do great spiritual works or to accept at the Hand of God the intuitive faculty of the highest order. But all who turn to God and know that He is a living Being in the world, are called from the place in which they manifest, to hold the light and to carry the light and power with them, using it where they are called to use it.

God is the living, vital, undying flame, the unquenchable power, the unquenchable burning fire in the universe – and that is the power of spirit. Through spirit is soul begotten, and because soul is begotten and directed to the physical body of man to fulfil his work in the material world, man brings to earth with him the Law of God and the Way of God and the full power of spirit which God has given him. He cannot go far along the path of life without being conscious of this flame within himself. He knows that it is something lit within him which draws him into the silence and the peace which he longs to touch, and yet material things call him aside and he allows – so often – the material world to overcome all his desires for spiritual progress and spiritual light.

132

The Initiation of Faith

The power of the living flame was given to you when your soul incarnated in matter. It was a very long time ago when that soul first came to earth. You have found your way through many incarnations and different ways of life in different classes of society – not for your own whim or selfish pleasure but in order that you should prove the existence of God to those with whom you come in contact. You cannot do that unless you have faith, unless you know and realise God within you, unless you can show your fellow-man God within him, to draw out, to strengthen and to uplift him.

You cannot touch the things of the material world without realising that they were given to you, and to all who use them, for the glorification of God. Man is called upon to use his love for God in service to Him, with the material gifts which are his to have and to hold. You cannot turn a blind eye to the darkness and therefore you must hold within yourself the living flame of the Holy Spirit, bright and strong, and clear and pure, to manifest the Love of God to your fellow-men.

What is your faith? Is it a faith which costs you nothing, or is it a faith which enables you to overcome all difficulties, to look for obstacles that you may pass them by and overcome them, to look for difficulties in the characters of the people you meet, that you may understand those characters and seek to guide them by the way of your own example? This faith does not seek to coerce people, nor to cover their way with material conditions and a way of life which is foreign to them and which you cannot accept, but to point to their foundation to show them that, though they build in matter, they are given those material trials to build for a spiritual purpose and to create God within themselves and within their work for Him.

This is what you are called to do, and not only to prove within yourself, within your heart, the very Being of God. For unless you do believe that God is within you, the silence, the meditation, the prayer and all that concerns it, means nothing to you or to any man round you. You must be able to accept the living flame of the spirit and to allow it to burn within your heart, to strengthen you

133

and to pour itself out through your eyes and your lips, that you may guide men towards peace.

We have spoken of the darkness in the world today and we have spoken of the great crisis in the heart of men, as in the world. The light wars with the darkness, and darkness would seem to gain the supremacy. And yet it does not gain supremacy, for light is ever stronger than darkness. As you – with your faith – bring light into your home, your circles, your places of work, so that light is carried by others and used and shed and strengthened because you have held it.

The Third Initiation – for which we take the symbol of the White Swan – is quite one of the most difficult initiations that we can touch. All day long, all the week long and the year long, we are tested and tried. Little material incidents are placed in our path as stumbling blocks by those who guide us, that we may overcome those incidents and, through the light, achieve power and greater light. For we touch the balance. Justice is represented at the centre of Libra in your chart. Look at your chart, find out where Libra comes on that map, consider the place and all that it means to you. Study the place in your own life and endeavour to follow it. For unless you can balance material with spiritual you cannot achieve the Third Initiation; which is perfect balance in perfect light – male/female, Adam/Eve. Adam, the male soul, Eve, with her intuitive faculty, her strength and power, proved by the Bible story perfect balance; male/female, perfect balance, soul/spirit/matter, spirit/matter/soul. All these things must be taken into consideration in your meditation and in your prayers.

In all you do and say and think, unless you yourself believe that God exists and is God, you cannot touch either the things of the spirit or the things of the world as you were meant to do when you came to earth to fulfil the path you are treading.

17. *Faith Without Works is Nothing Worth*

There is no attribute of grace so misunderstood and so misread by the children of the earth as faith.

Ponder upon those two sayings of the Master Jesus: 'Faith without works is nothing worth', and another one which was made during one of the most outstanding moments of His healing: 'Blessed are they who have not seen and yet have believed'.

In considering the cycle of evolution, we are conscious of the fact that our lives are planned before we come to earth, and that we prepare the plan of these lives in conjunction with those who come to guide us and in conjunction also with those groups of guiding spirits who, though remaining in the world of light, guide the fortunes of mankind. The man who comes back voluntarily to assist in some special work for the Father-Mother God always comes for a special purpose and works in a special plan – rather more special than the man who comes merely to fulfil his own Karma.

The time between incarnations is roughly two hundred years in your time, until man reaches a stage of evolution in which he comes to the point where there is no more compulsory incarnation for him. It is quite probable that he remains for a long while working in the planes of light, tying up those little knots of his material lives which must be tied and completed before he can close down his memory of them, and then he goes forward to a point where he will make some special study.

The Spiral of Life

When a great crisis is foreshadowed in the world of men, our Father-Mother God will call for volunteers, so that, in addition to those who are returning compulsorily to earth, there are a certain number who will come for a special purpose and they will take upon themselves their own karma, if there is any left to complete. That is a very small part of their life on earth. They will be the bearers of temple Karma, racial Karma and national Karma, and therefore they must gather together in groups according to the type of karmic disability which they have promised, or offered to fulfil.

The lives of such souls are never easy, and if you study their charts you will find that they are usually heavily afflicted by Saturn. In addition to that, coming on the earth with such a tremendous spiritual purpose to fulfil, either as teachers or healers or leaders, and political leaders are frequently among such souls, they will find themselves constantly beset with evil.

When the Master Jesus said: 'Blessed is he that hath not seen and yet hath believed', He was speaking of a particular group of men and women who came into incarnation during the troubled period of the Piscean age, to fulfil work for the Father-Mother God which had been planned in their life in the planes of light, but who had accepted the particularly difficult point that they had come to earth with the memory of that period of planning shut away from them.

It is often thus. There are those who return, not blind with the physical eye but blind in the spirit. It is for these the greatest possible test, where all memory of the glory of God would for a while be obliterated, that they should find themselves on earth without knowing – the knowing which means knowing of the Spirit – anything but the path which they have to tread.

'Blessed are they which have not seen and yet have believed'. Those great souls who, ploughing through the darkness in physical earth, yet can believe in God, in His power, in His love, in His strength and His light. 'Blessed are they that have not seen yet have believed.'

It does not mean that anyone who is blind and does not see the way is one of these mighty souls. These souls have come to prepare the world for a new Christ, to carry it through depths of suffering and misunderstanding by the very power of God which is working through them towards that goal of preparation, which holds the coming of the Aquarian Christ. They bring with them great light, which is given to them to light the paths of other men, to show the way of God to man. That light is given through the power of healing, through the power of teaching, through the love of God poured out through the teaching of the Master Jesus into the soul of living man today.

They walk amongst you, all unknowing who they are, where they come from and what their service is. But they have prepared a path for themselves which they are endeavouring to help mankind to follow, and that path rests on those other words: 'Faith without works is nothing worth'. They have come to hew the path by the sweat of their brow, to grow strong in the power of God, expressed through the power of material life, to learn to build for themselves a sure foundation, that their feet may rest securely upon the path which they are treading. Not that they may walk more smoothly and more easily for their own benefit, but so that they may draw to themselves a greater power of light, and through that greater power of light shed a beam on the path which mankind treads.

Those who come from the world of Spirit to guide you see that path of life clear before you and they see mankind rushing along it. Men with their eyes down, glued to the ground beneath their feet, gathering here and there, from the mud and the filth on which they tread, particles of gold which they rub between their palms to cleanse, and place within their pockets, that the gold may accumulate and they may hold it. As they run they hold their hands upon their pouches, in case the man behind them places his hand within and drags their ill-gotten gain from them. These have no faith. They move forward like blind creatures upon the path. Their eyes are fixed upon the soil, their hearts are closed within their breasts; anxious and fearful they move forward in case anyone shall take from them something which they want for themselves.

137

Beside them and around them move these great ones whose eyes are raised to the face of God, whose feet tread the path without faltering, whose light pours forth from hands and eyes and lips and pours down upon him who would grovel in the mire. Little by little the penetrating light from these souls reaches those blind ones who walk of their own free will in the darkness. For a while, perhaps, they are content to observe the light and to raise their eyes to touch the greater light beyond it. But always they are afraid of slipping back upon that miry path, and instead of placing their hand into the hand of the light-bearer, they stay awhile beside him and then leave him and, falling aside, take no more notice of the light.

Yet the light has spoken to them. It has shown them the way they can tread; it has shown them where they can cast aside all that prevents them from going forward free and clear and true. Here and there, there are some who stay the course. They have placed their hand in the hand of the light-bearer, moving onward and ever upward with him, treading with his pace. Learning step by step from him where to seek for light, they raise their consciousness and gain faith.

But none can go forward without a firm foundation. 'Faith without works is nothing worth.' The street sweeper who with his broom seeks out the tiny corner where the dirt and the rubbish lurk, a corner which will be overlooked by the overseer, and cleanses it, does not think of the overseer passing by. He remembers that a corner is clean and that he has made it clean. So it is with the child of God. He stretches out his hand to God and he knows that because he has swept and garnished that dark corner in a dark place, God will guide his feet, not for his own benefit to a palace, but to another corner even darker which the light of God will show him needs a greater cleansing. Perhaps ordinary men would say that such a one is going down in his own estimation and in the estimation of the world, because having learned to cleanse a little darkness he is guided to cleanse a greater one.

But that is not so, for his faith grows with each cleansing and purification, and the light becomes greater. If there are times when, in holding out his hand in the darkness, he is sore beset and tired, it does not mean that the light will fail him. He has faith to know that if his task is according to the will of God, God will bless him.

And there it is that so many students of spiritual things err and make mistakes. They do not submit their will to the will of God. Every task that you undertake should hold within your heart the thought: 'Is it the will of God that I shall do this, and do this in such and such a way, or am I pleasing myself and trying to please my fellowmen instead of pleasing God'?

18. *Joy*

Joy is a wonderful attribute of God and it is a very important attribute for all who heal, because without the knowledge of joy it is impossible to help the soul who is passing through depression or a neurotic condition of any sort.

We know that man has a physical body, a soul within which is the light of the holy spirit, and an etheric which is the covering for the soul – that etheric body within which lie the seven psychic centres or chakra and through which the light is held in the body of matter – and an astral body. We need to understand what the astral body really is. The astral body is not and cannot, at any time, be confused with the etheric because, although it is an exact copy, it is so entirely different that it is important that we do not confuse its function in any way.

Those who are clairvoyant, looking at the aura of a medium, speaker or teacher, will see a radiance surrounding such a one, which you can divide into many parts. After you have concentrated upon that aura for quite a period of time, with the eyes either open or closed, you will realise that, lying above the auric light emanation which you call the health aura and the aura of the etheric body, through which the light of the chakra shine, you will see what looks like partitions, or divisions, of light.

If you look more closely, these partitions will appear to be even as feathers and that is one of the great difficulties, for the clairvoyant, unless he is carefully taught and prepared, will be quite unable to realise that these feathers are feathers of light, and on many occasions he therefore describes this emanation of light as 'the head-dress of an American, North American or South American Indian'. It is very important to train yourself to distinguish between this light and the light which is shown as 'the head-dress of a North American or South American Guide'. This feather light is the light from the astral body.

The astral body has no function within the physical, such as supporting the etheric chakra, which belongs to the etheric body, or carrying the light of the spirit, such as the soul has, but the light of the astral body determines the destiny of the man. The light of the astral body is that radiance which links together mind, which is the organ of the soul, and brain which is the organ of the physical. Therefore the astral body carries, holds and attracts the light to the mind of man and through that attraction of light co-ordinates mind and body – the etheric and physical – although it does not have any function in the physical body beyond pouring radiance into the mind. That radiance is 'Joy'. The radiance which is controlled by the astral body of man is of that wonderful attribute of the Father-Mother God which is joy, and joy radiates the heart making it filled with glory and light.

Joy can govern the mind of man and through that governance of mind the whole man himself. Those who are healing with maladjusted children will find in many cases that when you apply the spiritual treatment laid down for such children in the right way, their eyes will light up for a short while and the whole being of the child becomes something quite different. That is due to the first entrance of joy, for the true Aquarian healer draws out and draws in the astral body of the sick child. That astral body, which can be covered over and completely darkened by physical suffering, can so lift the soul from physical suffering that the suffering is almost imperceptible to the child. That is true Aquarian healing. The children who are permitted to accept it are not always among those

142

whose physical lives are the longest. They may have come to earth for some karmic reason, some life to expunge, in which they took the joy of life from others. If so, as soon as they can radiate joy themselves, their mission on earth is fulfilled and completed.

The astral body is the first to disintegrate after death. It disintegrates when it is no longer necessary. It cannot manifest in the lower astral and, although the soul who would function after death on the lower astral plane would probably be unlikely to have developed his astral body, the astral body would be no use to him and would merely disappear. The soul who has gone forward far upon the path of life, whose astral body is so radiant that the whole aura is sparkling crystal feathers of light, will move so quickly through the shadow world into a plane of higher consciousness that he will have no need of the astral body after his journey. So we must distinguish carefully between the astral body and the etheric. The etheric body is the working man of the psychic centres, the astral body is the master or the ruler of the whole.

Joy is one of those attributes of God which are given to us pure and unadulterated as clear translucent light. That light is given to us as a direct force and it can only come to us if we earn it and if we prepare ourselves to receive it. No healer can give you the light of joy, unless you, yourself, first expand that light which is perhaps nothing but a glimmer in the astral body. The astral body is a body of glittering light and as such is the channel for the attribute of God that we call joy.

The radiance and beauty of joy leaves its mark on the children who know and understand how to take it and hold it. But it is denied altogether to certain groups or classes of the community who have not sufficiently prepared themselves to be channels for joy early in life. As they go forward to the fifties and beyond, they find themselves sometime a prey to depression and depressive neurosis of a more or less aggravated nature.

These neuroses are caused by one of four conditions. The first condition is guilt; the second condition is self-pity; the third is laziness and the fouth condition is misfortune.

143

Sometimes in our early days we have allowed a guilt complex to pervade our soul, our life. Then there has come a moment when that guilt has been poured deep down into the subconscious mind so that it is quite invisible on the surface of the mind and is known and belongs only to the soul who keeps it hidden. It can rise from time to time and cause an extraordinary mental sadness, mental sorrow, mental depression, but it is something even more serious than that. For as long as it remains in the subconscious mind, whether the subject is conscious or unconscious of it, it makes a barrier which is like a steel band around the astral body and that barrier prevents that wonderful feathery light from shining out from within the soul.

In other words, it cuts the mind away from the physical which is represented by the brain of the physical. Through that barrier and cutting away, the light cannot reach the physical body or the blood stream in the right way. Therefore, we can say that guilt can raise a barrier which can not only cause a depressive neurosis in the mind but can also seriously affect the digestive system and the condition of the physical body. The guilt complexes do not always belong to the soul himself; at times even they are inherited from the parents. They can be more easily handled and cured in early life but at all times they can only be helped if the neurotic person will go a very long way and be prepared to be very patient in the working out of this condition.

Sound, musical sound, or any sound in which the hands are occupied, such as the rhythmic sawing of wood, the hammering of iron, in which, of course, the will comes into play, all these things – digging the soil, heavy work on arable land, cutting down trees – all these things bring a certain relief for a time. But, above all, the exercise of retrospection must be used and in that exercise of retrospection gradually we see the barriers going down and the light coming in. For the astral body, whose blocking is the cause of the neurotic condition, is the channel for the light of the joy given by God.

The second condition which very rarely occurs except in early childhood, from about seven to fourteen, and then later in life, is self-pity. Self-pity raises an identical barrier but in rather a different way, because in self-pity the soul is drawing towards himself darkness and negation from the world of conscious thought. Even if that self-pity is only held within himself and is not projected upon the ether by the power of words and speech, it is nevertheless the dark barrier troubling and holding in chains the soul.

The astral body is a body of light which draws the light through the mind into the physical body and is the channel for the light of joy.

The third condition which can cause a barrier and which this time is a different coloured barrier altogether, is laziness. Anger, or jealousy, or spitefulness, those ugly thought forces, play no part in the astral body; they do not shut out joy. But laziness, or indolence, whether of body, or mind, can create such a barrier of steel that not only is the soul himself imprisoned behind barriers which all his shaking will not succeed in removing, but those bars raise a barrier, and a very formidable barrier, to the spiritually strong person who will try and help him. With laziness of mind you will nearly always find a stubborn resistance, a resistance to life, resistance to advice or knowledge of other people and a desire to remain shut up in his own little nest, little realising that the more he shuts himself in, the stronger and harder those prison bars grow and the more formidably they shut him in. The light of the spiritual soul within the barrier of the lazy, indolent person is of a strange dull green colour.

Our last category is lack of joy caused by misfortune. Misfortune can close down the channels of the body to the light of joy. You have come back to tread a path of life in which you are asked to fulfil certain karmic conditions, to repay debts which you have incurred in previous lives, to bring joy into the life of man through the joy in your own heart. But sometimes, through misunderstanding, you step aside from the path and then misfortune strikes you because you are out of tune with your own etheric pattern and moving among people who have no meaning for you and to whom you mean nothing. This is the moment when great strength of purpose and moral courage is needed to overcome it. But it can be overcome, and through that overcoming the light of joy will radiate through the channels of the astral body, which are closed down only so long as the soul sinks beneath his misfortune.

Part of the misfortune of man sometimes is in not understanding the change called death and, therefore, when a loved one is taken from him, he sorrows. You will even hear those who have passed over, and who are endeavouring to communicate with those they loved in the body, say that they cannot get near them for this barrier. What is that barrier? It is nothing but a power which prevents the body from opening out within the man and radiating light.

From the moment that the soul says: 'I will arise and go forward with courage and will try to see the hand of God in this blow which has come upon me,' from that moment the astral body opens and the light pours in. For the astral body gives nothing out. The light which is within the astral body is the light which pours in, for the astral body is but a channel for the glory of Joy.

19. *The Relative Importance of the Soul and the Personality*

Those who are interested in spiritual things should have an understanding of the part played by the soul, and the part played by the personality. The soul is that part of God to which God, Himself, gives light and life – God infuses the soul with the Holy Spirit, which is Himself. When the soul after each incarnation leaves the Place of Light, he returns to earth holding within his heart that measure of spirit which he has earned through his service to God. Part of that service is done in the spirit and, therefore, as a discarnate entity; part of it is done in the body and, therfore, as an entity incarnate in the flesh. As a discarnate entity the soul is free, unhampered, but it is a very different matter when the soul is born into a physical body, for he must face life from the angle of the personality.

Before you incarnate in the body you choose your personality. It is not a thing of a moment, you must return with the Servants of the Lords of Karma to study the chart of your previous lives. Through that chart you will learn where you have made certain mistakes; you will learn the importance of those mistakes which you must set about putting right at once, are mistakes; you will also learn that the most important of all mistakes which are made against another student, a fellow citizen, a member of your family. For mistakes which only hurt you yourself are bad enough, but mistakes which are made in such a way that they prevent others from sustaining the path of evolution, or cause them to stumble by the

147

way, are a very much more important matter than your own personal difficulties.

It is very wonderful to watch the discarnate soul being shown his mistakes. There is no question, when you are a discarnate soul, of covering up any mistakes. You will realise that your soul has tripped up, made certain errors of judgment, fulfilled a path which he was not meant to fulfil. You will be prepared, and probably interested, to check the amount of the disturbance you have caused, where you have caused it, and from what reason in your own self you have touched such difficulties.

Therefore, your next life must be planned with two or three points in mind. You will first of all be called upon to repay individual karmic debts, and for the repayment of those individual debts you will have to overcome certain obstacles of character, certain material obstacles upon the path which you are going to tread. Those material obstacles will force your personality either to stand aside from taking the test or force it forward.

The moment that we touch force we are touching effort, and the moment that we touch effort we are conscious that we are entirely involved in the personality. For in the soul there is no effort, but peace, love, dedication: that smooth movement of life which comes from the right development. But the personality is on earth to make an effort to overcome, to make an effort to build for the present, to make an effort to build for the future, and therefore the whole work of the personality is directed towards making an effort.

It is possible that the fear of death, or some great sorrow, or a conversation with a philosophical friend, may suddenly bring you to realise that there are things outside the material life of which you know nothing. If you are one of those people who want to be first, who want to emulate others and stand before them, you will immediately begin to enquire about these things to see whether there is anything there which will bring you into a front line. If you have belonged to some religious organisation which seems to have failed you, and you are seeking for a different way of life, you will be turned towards the religious devotional type of person who will

148

explain to you the things of the spirit. If you are seeking to use your mind to understand the work of God, to understand His Laws in the meaning of the universe, you will probably turn towards the author of these, without voicing the name of God and without wanting to touch any point of religion or belief.

Each one of those ways demands effort and, therefore, your soul which is guiding you pushes the personality forward and says, 'here is where you begin'; and you begin to enquire from the angle that appeals to you most. As soon as your enquiring mind lights up, those who guide you become very busy in the world of spirit – here is someone who is trying mentally to break through the etheric barrier which separates the world of spirit from the world of men, and they will encourage your effort by giving power to your soul through your personality.

To those of you who have studied the links between the soul and the personality, this may seem the wrong way round – but it is not. For you cannot unfold the power of the spirit and all that goes with it, you cannot learn to serve God as he expects you to serve Him, you cannot cleanse and purify your soul from the sins of the past, without coming to the point that you must set aside a time for development. By development I do not mean, for everyone, sitting in a development class – that is, perhaps, the easiest way of all.

Those of you who have read Gerald Heard's excellent little book, *Training for the Life of the Spirit*, will realise the importance of detail and, above all, the importance of the silence. In the world, your personality is surrounded with noise. Some of that noise is pleasant, some of it is unpleasant, all of it is creating a turmoil through which God cannot be heard. God is calling you into the silence, and as you try to obey His call you are conscious of a certain adjustment being made in your Life which is very surprising to you. You may begin these studies by sitting with a medium who will tell you, as far as he is permitted, what you are expected to do. But whether you sit with a medium, or attend a spiritualist service where you are given a message, or read Gerald Heard's book, they all point the same way – the call has gone out for you, your soul says: 'God is important to my work in the world of men — listen to me'.

It is possible that that call goes out some years before you take any notice of it at all. You may think that during that period of time nobody is bothering, but that fallow period is very often a period of great development. If you have been through one of those fallow periods, look back on it, check up on it, and see how, through easy and difficult stages, all the obstacles to your hearing the Voice of God have been removed from your path during a given period. You have only to hold up your hand and say: 'Here am I, Lord, call me', for the world of spirit is ready for you.

But the world of spirit sees a material path already planned with your personality, and it sees the difficult adjustment which the soul must make to guide that personality. Therefore, those who are going to work with you as your guides from the world of spirit, begin to pour power into your personality by strengthening it. Not to make the way easier — that is never the way of God — but to try and give you pointers along that way which will guide you from point to point.

You will find that as soon as you begin to notice that things seem to be shaping and turning so that you may really be free to study the esoteric wisdom, you are conscious of a much greater desire to say 'thank you', than you have ever felt before, and it is that first 'thank you' in the heart of your personality which breathes into yourself the very Breath of God. Then, at that moment, your aura lights up. Only when your aura is completely alight can your doorkeeper and your spiritual guide really approach you.

If you could picture the difficulties that the doorkeeper and the spiritual guide have in guiding your personality to this very point, you would realise how important it is in the early stages of development to place yourselves entirely in the hands of God — to be fluid, easily moved where He wants you to go and able to hear His Voice. The personality grows stronger and begins, much more hopefully, to look back over the day and perhaps find a few minutes in the morning and a few minutes in the evening, which can be given to God. The soul draws nearer; and where the personality is backed by your two guides and your own effort to succeed, the soul is backed by the very Light and Love of God.

The soul moves very slowly, he must fit himself entirely into your own aura. The colours that he brings must be entirely harmonious and sympathetic. He must never project those colours, or those rays, in such a way as to cause you unhappiness or disease, for very much disease can come from an inharmonious approach of the soul, or too swift an approach of the soul. For when the power of radiation brought by the soul is too strong for the personality, it upsets the balance of the subject himself. Many of the cases of Epilepsy and Petit Mal which we are touching today are due to that very point – that the soul rushes in too quickly at the call of the personality and causes almost an inflammatory condition of the rays between them.

The soul does not want the personality to form a barrier. He must be able to move forward and back to the personality, controlling and guiding him. That guidance must come from the soul itself, for the soul is directed by the plan of life which you have made with him. That plan of life now begins to assume very important proportions. The personality has first had to make the effort to reach the soul; he does that by prayer, meditation, thanksgiving. As soon as he has made the effort the soul comes forward, for the soul is a gracious giver and he brings such power and light as is necessary for the next step.

You will find, at this point in your training, that you will be very sensitive to the opinions of others. Your soul is not entirely in control of the personality, the personality is beginning to feel that it must reach the soul, and there is a no-man's-land in between. For the moment, therefore, you will be swayed by the mind and the thought of your friends, and very often when we draw near to such a soul we find them saying: 'you won't', 'you will', 'you won't' – not knowing in the least which way to go, which way to turn. The only cure for that is silence. Go into the silence, prepare that silence, let

151

there be a gramophone record or some beautiful music on the radio, or a religious service on the radio.

You are dependent upon all those souls with whom you come in contact during the day for many of your steps in life. If one of those souls fails, the plan must be altered, so for a while you feel yourself in the balance, you don't know whether to go to the right or whether to go to the left, or whether to stand quite still and wait. You believe – because you have come to believe at this stage – that God guides the plan of your life, and unless you in yourself are able with absolute truth to say: 'I have stepped out of the plan of my life, I must stand still', you will be moving from one side to the other, making this mistake and that mistake.

It is just at the moment that the plans of your life have to be altered through the action of your fellows, that you find it a consolation and a help to talk out your difficulties with someone else. You will find that there are certain conditions in the plan of life which are alike for yourself and for the person you choose to talk to. You may even find that one or two of the faults which you have been fighting ever since you started your development, are identical faults in your friend, and that that friend may have gone further along the path of conquering these faults, or he may not be so far along as yourself. Move very slowly in these conditions, hasten nothing. I would like to see those words 'hasten nothing' written over the forehead of everyone who is seeking to study the things of the spirit to work as healers, to do work in sanctuaries and places where we prepare the way of God.

Because it is that standing still which is essential. When you stand still you can make contact, and those who are nearest to you are always your own two guides, your doorkeeper and your spiritual guide. Therefore it is to them we turn – we say: 'this student is not making the pace, he has fallen behind in a second or third examination, he has lost his foothold, he is impatient, he is not waiting, he is not giving us the moment of peace in which we can adjust these matters'. So very often a complete break must be made in the life of the student, so that all these things begun on an entirely different basis may be strengthened and overcome in the personality under the guidance of the soul.

20. *Changing Conditions as the Age of Aquarius Approaches*

There are certain conditions under which we work, which should give us a totally different attitude towards life and living conditions from anything that we have touched hitherto. If we look at our works of art, our architecture – and in fact at anything which is prepared at great expense of time and thought and money for the betterment of the world – we shall realise that there is one thread running through everything, and that is the thread of the personality. For the personality of men is reaching a crisis, and when a crisis occurs in the world of men, every planet, every star, every tiny speck of light in the firmament is affected by that crisis.

We shall find more men and women interested in and anxious to help animals than we have ever seen before. Because animal life is reaching a crisis of elimination, a point where the animals who have been loved by the human race and have made good friends among the human race and continued their evolution, will be separated from those who are still in a savage condition and consider only the welfare of their own bodies, if they consider that at all.

There are, mingling among the dark-skinned races of today, many young souls in their first step in evolution. But there are also young souls among the white races, and therefore the fact that certain young souls are coming into incarnation in the savage races is a step forward in the history of native evolution.

Beside those young souls in the dark-skinned bodies, there are many animal incarnations which have no soul at all. You may think that it is impossible for a man to exist only with a personality. But these men are definitely less than the animal creation that is loved and understood by man. They will not, of course, take animal shape as many people still believe. They will be human beings and they will be medically of great strength, and probably we should say almost of valour. For it is only a mismanaged soul that knows fear by the personality itself, and does not accept or hold fear within his heart.

These incarnational changes are not accidental. We have arrived at a point in the evolution of the Earth, in the evolution of the etheric planes, in the evolution of the stars and the planets, when all these things shall be brought together and each shall give of its substance of Light or Darkness to the other. We ask ourselves, in loving these animals and caring for them and setting them out on a path which is totally different from the animals which have not been loved and cared for by man, are we placing their feet in danger? Is it for us to protect and hold them back? To a certain extent we must always protect those we love, whether they be of the animal kingdom, the kingdom of nature such as the trees and the flowers, or even the rivers and the great waters which also have the power of the Spirit of God flowing through them. But we must realise that at no time is any of this conditon brought to fulfilment without the plan of the mind of God behind it. Therefore, we must endeavour to see how and when and where the mind of God is working through us to assist us to take our place in this great period of evolution.

In art and architecture we realise that the world is going through a period of transition. A period when men are being called upon to function in very small spaces, in box-like rooms, and buildings where there would seem to be no luxury and no spiritual light.

Just as we are called upon, through our love, to help in the regeneration of the animal kingdom, so we are called upon to infuse with a new light these buildings and resting-places which to us seem square and ugly. If they were made with great beauty we should find there was no place for this new vibration of light which is being

154

poured towards us. We should find also that we should ourselves sit back and saturate ourselves with the beauty which we have created, forgetting that creation is the work of God, and that God creates by the power which man gives Him, and that through that power new worlds will come to light.

We are accustomed to consider man as having five senses and the paranormal sense as a sixth sense. But it is not, and it cannot be a sixth sense. It is a spiritual sense granted by God to man who has earned it and the use of it, through his work in service in former lives. Therefore it is a sense which is rarely touched by those whom we call new souls – the new soul being man in the body who has come into incarnation for the first, second or perhaps third time, and now returns to make good what he destroyed and damaged and hurt in his previous lives – and it is a sense which is not touched by those who are incarnated without the soul.

All round you, you are seeing destruction and it seems to run through all classes, all communities, beginning with the thirteen and fourteen-year-olds who destroy railway carriages and lights, and other things which are of vital importance to man. And you wonder: 'Are they not destroying these things because they are no longer things of our present life'? No, that wave of destruction must come into being at the same time as, around the destroyers, there is being woven a web of Light which will eventually separate them from those who build constructively. Whether they destroy what is ugly or what is beautiful, whether they even take away life, they are still being used by certain forces which have to be released in this day of time to clear away certain conditions of the old world and to rebuild, upon the foundations destroyed, a new world of new beauty, a new harmony and a new strength.

In various spiritual Centres there will be found many who are able to be used as instruments for the use of that sense of the Spirit. There are others who feel that they are not developing as they should do and are asking why, and you will find that those who are not developing are usually, not always, still completely wound up in their own personality. They differentiate between right and wrong

155

from the material angle of man which they have been taught from their cradle, but they do not see the change that is coming to the world. They have very little vision for the colour and the Light of the Spirit, and they remain held in the bondage of the personality without setting it free.

Freedom is the keynote of the new incoming Christ and, as we all know, we can only be free when we are completely self-disciplined. The youngsters who damage the railway carriages, tear down the railings and knock down old ladies, are not free. They are in bondage to the Spirit of Darkness which urges them forward. They have no vision of the things of the Spirit, and therefore they have no ability to use that wonderful sense of the Spirit which man will need to use more and more in the coming days. To some of us it may come only in old age, but it will come – it must come and it must be part of life.

We watch the hooligans endeavouring to break their chains in bondage to the Evil One, by destroying all that life means to their fellows. Some of these hooligans are very young souls but they all have had previous incarnations and there will come a time when they will look at what they are doing with totally different perception. That perception must come from people, who, having learned about it, having accepted it, knowing the joy and the beauty of the things of the Spirit, are able to talk and tell about the glory of life through life, not the life of destruction. We have not yet finished with the destruction; it must go on until the time comes when those who destroy have no longer the desire to destroy. In many cases they seek power, they seek self-aggrandisement, they are showing-off. But in many other cases it is the Darkness working within them, rousing their turbulent blood. This is almost equal to the savage without a soul, not caring for the consequences.

We are preparing with a much greater understanding for the coming of the Christ of Aquarius. It is not a question of a moment of arrival or of an appointed day or time; it will happen when men's hearts are ready. It will be prefaced, not by the taking of a census in order to bring the right people together, but by the mingling of East and West in harmony, love and understanding; by the approach of those who have learned in their schools and colleges to discipline their souls, and through the soul's discipline to guide the personality.

We shall each be given some special task to fulfil for God in the way of Aquarius. We are not allowed to know of these things of the Spirit, and of the self-discipline which they involve, without passing them on to others. Therefore we shall find that, from time to time, souls who are of great importance in the road of the New Christ will be sent to us, that we may teach them that inner discipline of Light which they lack, and teach them the meaning of the path of the soul and its purpose in the world of men today.

Great changes will come, with the rushing of mighty waters. The sea, as well as the ocean, would seem but a small water compared to the vast waters which must precede the Age of Aquarius and act as cleansing streams. You may find that certain waters running under your own homes and buildings must be turned aside, in order to further this cleansing process. You may find that you yourself will be drawn into a study of water and water conditions, and wonder why this has suddenly opened a door for your study.

Over and over again the cleansing waters will mean more. Man will find that where he is called to guide and discipline the young, to wash even under the cold water which passes through the pipes and taps in your own houses will be an absolute necessity. Where you have an unpleasant taks to fulfil, wash your hands first under a running tap, and you will find the water will act as a courage-giving agent. You will be called upon to listen, for the waters of Aquarius must be heard, and they can only be heard on the vibration which we call 'paranormal'. The vibration of the ethers of Light, vary in intensity from the denser ethers of the astral plane adjoining our own plane of Earth, right through the other astral planes one after the other, to the Garden of Remembrance, where every tree and every stream and every movement will speak to you. Those planes of consciousness lie beyond the seventh plane of the astral, planes to which you raise your consciousness,

157

becoming more sensitive to the sound around you, more sensitive to the music of the spheres and through that sensitivity stronger, better, clearer, purer for the work which you are called upon to do.

The astral planes have their place and their purpose. Voice mediumship and even certain forms of astral trance mediumship are fast disappearing and will be heard no more. They have done their part, they have filled the life of man and in many cases have given hope to the mourner, and love and understanding to the soul that mourns. But that is passing. The moment is come when man must use his own consciousness to find the beauty of God in which his soul delights.

The things of the past hold much of the Spirit and the Power of God. Where you handle them, where you touch them, where you contemplate them, you must do so first by cleansing them with the Light of the Spirit, that they may not hold the vibrations of Power and Darkness and ugliness with which life has smirched and spoiled them. You will learn to look behind that smirching and spoiling for the true spirit of the beauty of art, for the true sound of the note of the voice of God, which sounds rightly every time a musical sound is placed upon the ether.

Treat the Darkness and the ugliness through which we are passing with positive thought, in the knowledge that your thought can turn that very ugliness of life into the beauty which you can touch through your unfoldment of your paranormal consciousness and the translation of that paranormal consciousness into the consciousness of the Most High.

The service you are giving, the work you are about to fulfil, whether to your earthly masters or to your heavenly Master, is not accidental. Every time that you need guidance, help and knowledge, God will give it to you, provided you in your turn give back to God the service you have come to fulfil for Him, and with Him, in preparing the way of the New Christ of Aquarius.

21. *The Blue Light of Aquarius*

The Light of Aquarius is blue – a very deep and unusual blue, warm and yet cool, in fact almost ice-cold in its strength – and the closer it draws to the children of men, the greater the warmth and the less is the density of its colour. The deeper colour touches the spiritual planes of consciousness and so only results in touching the tip of the aura of the individual who is tuned-in to those planes of Light. It is like a shaft, and when you see in the Christmas picture the great star over Bethlehem mirrored, notice that it frequently has what we can only call a tail stretching from its height in the heavens to the Earth itself. That is the right description for this radiant blue light which is centred through Aquarius and emanates from the planet Jupiter.

You will find it strange that Jupiter, who represents all that is beneficent in human nature, who brings the desire for giving, for Truth, for beauty, should at this moment become as one who is not a giver. But we must remember that the first important contact that any planet makes with the Earth-plane is always fraught with uncertainty and frequently with disharmony. Other planets and signs which are in the ascendant at this moment show a very disturbed world of men, and that disturbance does not emanate from the heavens but from the inner heart of man himself. Where man has conquered and is conquering the Darkness, the ray of light which goes forth to meet the great ray of Jupiter is valuable indeed to all of us who seek the regeneration of mankind.

It is one of the strange points in the evolution of man that as soon as anyone talks or thinks of a troubled period in life, there are so many who want to evade the troubles and lose themselves, either on a planet far away or in some corner of the Earth where they think that the Darkness cannot touch them. When you have an earthquake or a volcanic eruption in a country, it brings sorrow and tragedy and death and destruction, but after that destruction is completed, man only seeks to reconstruct and rebuild the world which has been shattered around him. Look at Hiroshima, how it was shattered, how its people are still suffering from the appalling effects of that terrible bomb, and yet the city has been rebuilt and in many places is a thing of beauty, and the people are working and striving to bring harmony of life and, where disharmony has reigned, to bring Light in its wake.

Perhaps we shall not see in the East the extraordinary industrial troubles which we are going to face in Europe, and in this country especially. Because while men are endeavouring in this country to escape from the result of their evil ways and their folly, they can only achieve rebuilding when they raise their consciousness to God. If they are not yet ready for the power of the consciousness to be planted within them, then they remain static in a state of quiescence, agreeing with all that is happening in the world but without blaming themselves or thinking at any point that anything that they have said or done could have brought about a ghastly crisis.

Crises we must have and we must ask ourselves, have we really done the work which God sent us into this world to do? Have we really brought harmony among the nations, harmony among the people, harmony in all things? Nature is harmonious, but man has sought to destroy nature at every point. The birds and the animals, and all the living creatures which God gave man for his joy and companionship, have been ruthlessly destroyed at his hands and there is only a minimum of the population of these islands who endeavours at any point to save the destruction of animal life.

There are wonderful philosophers, there are great nature lovers, but they are still in the minority. Always at the back of the fight which they are putting up to preserve nature and the creatures, there is the horror that as fast as they achieve life, man is engulfing nature in death and suffering. It is not so much death that we blame – it is the suffering caused, which is so unnecessary and so unneeded, even for man's advancement.

Look into your own lives and ask yourselves what you are doing that is constructive. Are you building a way of life which many men will seek to follow? Are you beginning at the beginning with the life of the child, and building Truth and honesty with these children where Darkness and untruth so often surrounds them in their homes and in the world? Are you building in your midst a place of Light where men will come with joy and happiness, and rest in the silence? Are you endeavouring to fulfil your own life so that your physical and etheric bodies may be ready for the transplanting of this great and glorious Ray which shines as a star in the firmament before the Coming of the New Christ?

People say: 'Why? Why is the Coming of this Christed One delayed? Why does He not come now, while we are here on Earth to accept Him?' We did not come to Earth into incarnation to receive Him – or very few of us. We came to Earth to prepare the way for Him, to bring generosity and kindliness and love into the world, that the whole path on which He travels may be a path of Light.

There are great changes at work in the world but the rulers of the nations find it difficult to make decisions. They are living in a world making contacts with the children of the people, whose only idea perhaps is self-advancement, strength of purpose to endure and build and enjoy more and more fruits of their labour. But every time there is an addition to the wealth of the individual there is a taking away of the necessities of life from someone else, and that is why you face a world in which so much poverty, so much starvation and human misery is to be seen on every side. That is balance. As one man gives and another takes, so is the balance

161

perfect in the eyes of God, but when man goes on grasping and taking, and grasping and taking more and more of the world's goods at the hands of the power of the Spirit, more starvation, more suffering must come into the life of man before the perfection of balance may be achieved.

Each year we have dwelt in thought upon Christ Jesus, the Christ of the Piscean Age, who not only undertook to teach man how to live, how to bring harmony into his life, but how to avoid conflict and the causing of death to his fellowman. Now, however, we are touching very closely the great blue Light of Aquarius. It will not draw close to the Earth in the way that the Star of Bethlehem drew near, for the time is not yet ready for the Earth to accept it, but little by little as the years advance we shall notice that certain leaders of various groups in the Western world will be called together in spiritual conference.

We are not referring to the government of nations but to those many souls who have been prepared to accept the power of this Ray, and to reduce it and transmute it to those who are ready to touch it. Therefore the Star of Bethlehem at Christmas will be twofold: the star of Light which belongs to the Piscean Age, and the somewhat weaker star of the Aquarian Age which belongs to the new Christ.

When we are conscious of these great stars coming together we shall know by our feelings whether we are called towards Aquarius or whether we remain static in Pisces. Not many will feel they want to remain in Pisces. Many will want to go forward, they want to see the way that they are going, that they may take others along that way. They want to know how to teach and to speak and to govern not only themselves, but the younger souls who walk beside them.

In order to do that, they must accept the full teaching of the Piscean Age and hold it in their hearts until the heart becomes enlarged with the love which they give to God, and in that love the Aquarian ray is born. It is a great and mighty ray, divided into so many lesser rays, in order that it may touch and enter the groups which are studying for the coming of the New Christ. It is a ray of

162

such magnitude and strength that a tiny thread of it can destroy a world and send it shuddering to the bottom of the ocean. That is a world in which we hope we have no part, for we believe that our place is here on Earth and that wherever we are taken during our journey on Earth it is by the Will of God.

Sometimes we tread aside from the path, also by the Will of God, in order to learn some lesson which we have failed to learn in the past, and always at our heart's door there hammers justice, truth and purity. These are the points of modern man, which he must remember before he can pass from the teaching of the Christian era to touch the teaching of the New Christ.

Those who come in the full knowledge that they are to be channels for those words which are to come forth from the Christed One, will have and hold the things of the Spirit in reverence. They will play their part in service, realising, wherever they are called to serve, that service is an advancement not only in the physical world but in the spiritual. Where they play their part in that service, they will be called upon to do and undertake greater and greater tasks, until the whole world will ring with the glory of their being.

Every time you accept a service in a Sanctuary such as any of the Sanctuaries over the world, you are conscious of an inner glow which, in reality and in a few words, is God saying: 'Thank you'. When you feel that inner glow you know that the path that you have chosen, however difficult and full of difficulty, sorrow and unhappiness it has been, is definitely the one which your feet are right in treading.

'Things then will be made plain for you.' Not all things, for you still have years to remain on Earth and that would be too long a test for your memory, but little by little, to show you where your place lies in the Age of Aquarius. To show why you are here, why you fulfil certain tasks, many of which are probably uncongenial, in order that you may carry the power of Aquarius through yourself into the ways of God. That is the great lesson for the coming of a Star – the Light goes from God, is sent forth by God at His Hand.

The Spiral of Life

Whoever is ready to touch that Light will receive it in great measure, but he must never hold the bearer – he must let the bearer go.

22. Succeeding Ways of Thought on the Rays of the Masters

If you study the history of religion you will find that certain cruel practices were fulfilled in every age under the name of the power of God. Cruelty reached its apex in that period of time known as the Inquisition, and so great was the suffering of those whom the persecutors tried to force into a way of thinking which they could not accept, that the Father-Mother God, Himself, withdrew further into His place of light, and placed round Himself a Group of Masters who were later chosen to guide the life of man in preparation for the new Christ of Aquarius.

During the period which succeeded the Inquisition, the hatred died down very slowly and the cruelty slowly but surely ceased. There came an age throughout the world, except in India and China, of great licence. And following that licence, there grew out of that reaction the hard bigotry of the Victorian, if we think of it as English, and if we think of it as Continental, the harsh bigotry of a Protestant faith which was a complete swing of the pendulum from the Inquisition.

There were faults in both ways of thinking, and just as the Catholics tried to force men into their belief, so the Protestants, and the various Churches which broke away from the Protestant Church in that day of time, persecuted people who did not believe as they did. They persecuted them not on the physical plane as the inquisitors did, but on the mental plane. So first there was the physical suffering of the Inquisition, and then the mental suffering under the bigoted belief in hellfire and the devil and eternal damnation which came in during the Victorian Era.

Many men broke away from those bigoted beliefs and founded softer, gentler ways which led them nearer to God. But even they felt that God was afar off and they must seek to draw Him nearer by their way of life, which should be modelled on the Brotherhood of Man and the Doctrine of Love. During this period there came into being a sect of gentle, quiet people whom you know now as the Quakers. They believed that it was necessary to link in with the spirit of the Most High in order to hear the Will of God for man.

But about the same period of time, when the Father-Mother God was more withdrawn than He had ever been, a command went forth from Him that certain Masters should leave the place of light where, in a circle, they surrounded Him, and that they should descend slowly but surely towards the earth plane in order to bring to these darknesses those greater rays of light which should guide the future of mankind.

The Master Hilarion went forth on the sound of the announcing trumpet, and came to earth with what would seem a harsh and cruel message, for he brought the message of agnosticism. The Father-Mother God said: man has tried to prove my cruelty, both on the physical plane and on the mental plane, now he shall learn what it means to walk in the darkness and find Me not.

So it is about that Victorian period that you find many men attending Church, and apparently worshipping God, who do not accept God at all, who do not believe in His love nor in His power. And from that came out the man who said there is no God, creation is a process of nature, and when asked how nature began the process, he endeavoured to prove it on scientific lines which departed from God. Once man had left the ways of God and no longer looked for His help or His guidance, no longer accepted the worship and humility which were His due, he began to be afraid. Part of the threat of the punishment of hellfire held sway here, and part of the suffering was due to the immense loneliness which man felt when he had no God.

So out of agnosticism the Master Hilarion drew a ray of light which should cast out fear, and in the hearts of men he planted the seed of knowledge which proved survival after the death of the body, and through the proof of survival He took away from man the fear of death.

Not very long after, the Master Moria and the Master Koot Hoomi were sent forth by the Will of the Father-Mother God. They saw that the beauty of the Spiritualist faith which had been created by the Master Hilarion was being dragged in the dust and in the mire of superstition and untruth. They brought into being all the force of the light which they were permitted to touch and to hold, and they found a channel for their teaching in a simple Russian woman who is known to you as Madame Blavatsky, the Founder and Leader of the Theosophical Movement. The Theosophists of those days accepted life after death as a change from one state of consciousness to another, and they decried the psychic manifestations of the Spiritualists, dragging them out into the daylight and warning the world against them. Those who belonged to the Spiritualist Movement realised there was much which Madame Blavatsky had to give and they endeavoured to leave their astral psychic manifestations behind them, to rise through the astral to a greater study of esoteric matters, to accept the guidance of Divine Beings ordained by God to guide mankind.

Then another Master went forth and he showed up the faults in the Theosophical Movement and the Spiritualist Movement. He guided into the view of man a channel known as Mrs. Baker Eddy, who spent her life trying to prove that much which had gone before was mortal sin. Again this new ray of light showed up the darkness in the older way of thinking and many turned towards Mrs. Eddy and her teaching called Christian Science. For each leader took a portion of what was best in the old belief and, moulding it and preparing it with a greater light, gave it as a new glory to the children of men.

We have considered these beliefs and ways of thinking in terms of Western teaching, but there were changes going on in the East at the same time and many of these changes were made manifest in the Western teachings. For the work of these Masters was to work together for good, which is God, and they knew that when the truth really was made manifest in the heart of man, there would be no need for Theosophies and Religions, but only the one law, the Law of God. They knew that that could only come into being when man had probed through unbelief, through fear of the unknown, through hidden mysteries, through the knowledge of sin and all that it meant, and taken from each a little light which he would mould together in the true Temple of Light into which the Father-Mother God would direct the ray of the Christ of Aquarius.

Many years have passed since these Masters, with their great methods of changing and mixing up and sifting the dross from the gold, began their journey through the planes towards the earth plane. As they grow nearer, the heart of man is raised, the light within the heart begins to glow and shine to without, until the whole aura of man is one glory of light. It is that light which God needs from all his children which will make it possible for the Masters to stand aside and, with their raised arms, to prepare the archway through which the Father-Mother God Himself will tread towards the earth.

That light which you are being taught to prepare is based upon love, not the emotional love of the personality but the deep, true love of the soul. For until you have realised and accepted and given forth your whole being as love, your soul cannot be liberated, and so long as your soul is tied to the karmic wheel, it must return, and return, to fulfil the journey of life.

All those who tread this path as disciples of the Great White Brotherhood have already raised their consciousness from the sixth plane of the astral to the seventh plane of the place of light – the Garden of Remembrance – but they must pass through the sixth plane. It is not possible to touch the seventh plane, with its occult esoteric teaching, unless you have yourself accepted and known the way of the Spiritualist.

168

For the work of the Spiritualist is to cast out fear, to help the mother who is left alone to bring up her family; to know that the husband she loved is so close to her that he can guide her in everything she does, even as if he were here in the flesh with her; to help those children who sorrow for their parents to know that they are not completely friendless or alone, but that those very parents who have grown in the spirit beyond the earth plane can give them power and light to see the way ahead of them. To take away fear from life and to replace fear by love is the work of the teacher and the work of the healer, and all who have that divine touch, either upon their lips or within their finger tips, know what it means to contact the ray of the Master Hilarion.

We have now left the things of the sixth plane of the astral behind us and we are developing on the seventh plane, which is mental mediumship. We realise that in that plane no untruth can live, no darkness, no shadow of turning but that the knowledge and the wisdom which we shall receive there is something which we can apply to our own daily lives to the building of the Kingdom of God in the hearts of men.

23.   The Hierarchy of Heaven

We are going to consider the Hierarchy of Heaven and the High Heavens in which our Father-Mother God rests upon His Throne of Glory.

The Throne is not like an earthly throne. It is set above the clouds, above the heights, so that it appears to be very far away even to the Seven Spirits around the Throne. The Throne consists of the Trinity, that is, of the Father-Mother and the Son. From this Trinity spread forth the power and the light of the Seven Rays. The colours of these rays in High Heaven are indescribable. But when we have left this place of holiness we shall consider colours from an earthly angle. From the Throne, from the Trinity, ray forth the power of the Seven Rays to the Seven Ray Lords.

These are not tiny shafts of light. They are immense and powerful beams of light and their radiance enfolds the whole of the Seven Ray Lords and the Seven Spirits before the Throne. The Seven Spirits before the Throne move on a lower level than the Throne of God Himself. They are gathered before the Throne; they do not surround the Throne. They are gathered before the Throne so that, in a sense, these Seven Spirits are on a level with the Footstool of the Father-Mother God.

There are Seven Ray Lords. These Seven Ray Lords accept the power of the Seven Rays from the Father-Mother God and transmit it to the Seven Spirits round the Throne, who rest upon a lower level of consciousness than the Seven Ray Lords.

171

The power of the Rays is transmitted from the Father-Mother God direct through the Seven Ray Lords, who transmit it direct to the Seven Spirits round the Throne. It is they who hold it and decide whether it shall be lessened in power and light for its next journey through the Seven Lesser Spirits.

The Seven Lesser Spirits are still around the Throne. They do not move at the back of the Throne; they remain around before the Throne. They are responsible for the power which is transmitted by means of the Rays to man, and through them we touch the Seven Types of Man and the Seven Root Races.

Below the Seven Ray Lords are the Seven Spirits before the Throne, and then the Seven Lesser Spirits who are responsible for the Seven Types of Man and the Seven Root Races.

Although these are lesser spirits it is they who give the decision, the amount of power and light which can be given to these seven types of man and to the seven root races, for they hold the creative force of the Father-Mother God and that creative force governs birth and death.

Then on a lower level of consciousness we find the Seven Sub-Spirits, linked directly with man himself through the seven chakra of the physical body. Therefore, the rays transmitted from the Seven Ray Lords are eventually accepted by each one of the Seven Sub-Spirits and transmitted through the chakra of spiritual man, thus linking spiritual man as an individual through his chakra, through the Seven Lesser Spirits, through the Seven Spirits round the Throne to the Seven Ray Lords, and thus direct to God.

Whereas the Seven Lesser Spirits use one ray for each type of man and one ray for each of the seven root races, the Seven Sub-Spirits combine the use of all Seven Rays in the body of one man. It is difficult to understand, but it is the Seven Sub-Spirits who use the sublimated power of the rays altogether. That is why it is so important for the student of development to move very, very slowly if he is to unfold his consciousness and use his soul in the right way.

You make no contact with those Seven Sub-Spirits until you have first been linked by your Third Guide and placed into the right position in your type of man and according to your root race. It is of the utmost importance that your physical body should be cleansed and purified, so that no block occurs in the physical which can prevent the rays passing through to your etheric body, into the bloodstream and into your seven centres.

In addition to the power of the Seven Rays, we must remember that within the Hierarchy are seven great divisions. Each of these divisions is governed by its own ray and Ray Lord and draws its power direct from its Ray Lord. The power used by the Hierarchy of Heaven is love, whatever the colour of your ray or the ray which governs your type, or your group, or your Root Race.

The root race has nothing to do with the race of mankind; It is not an indication that you are a Russian or a German. Your Root Race is a spiritual division which concerns the moment of the birth of your soul, the moment of its first coming to earth to be born into a physical body, and the achievement of its first life on earth after it has returned to the world of spirit.

Under the domination of the Seven Ray Lords we have Seven Divisions in the Hierarchy and these Seven Divisions are known as Ashrams. The word 'Ashram' is a word of power and should never be lightly used to describe a material condition. You may build a centre, you may build a Temple, you may build a Sanctuary, and all these may be blessed by the Father-Mother God and His love poured out upon them so that they grow in spirit and in strength, but only the Ray Lord builds an Ashram.

Every Ashram has its leader. The leaders are very rarely given names in material life or material words. They are known as Chohans, and if a distinction is needed other than the colour ray which they control, they are given a number. The number means nothing at all in the world of spirit but it is a distinction in the mind of man.

Therefore each Ashram gathers together its groups of Masters. These Masters, in their turn, control groups of souls. Some of these souls will be in the world of spirit, others will be in the physical body of flesh. The only control that is used by the Chohans is love,

173

and love can cause the light of God to shine through his ray, through the seven types of man of the seven root races.

The Masters meet each in their own Ashram and they are in their turn each linked with seven groups. Therefore each Ray Lord has seven groups of Guides who are leaders and who control their own groups of Twelve. If you follow a leader, the Third Guide of that leader will be on a higher level of consciousness than the leader of the Ray Group of Twelve, and each member of that group will be the Third Guide of one of the Twelve members of your group which links with that particular leader.

Therefore every earthly group should have twelve members and one leader, the leader using in his speech, that is sound, and in his work, the power of the Seven Rays. Each member of the group should function upon one ray.

The colours of the rays in earthly language are red, blue, yellow, the three principal pure colours, and violet, green, orange and white. White is the colour of love, and although love permeates all the other rays it comes to its fulfilment in the white ray.

There are subsidiary rays, and in every group of twelve there must be five subsidiary rays which are composed of a mixture of colours, with the addition of the white ray.

When referring to the white ray in this connection, we do not mean the Christ ray. The white ray is no more important than any of the other six rays. The important ray is that powerful ray which, containing all seven rays, is the powerful strong light of your own Ashram.

Students of spiritual philosophy belong to a group of twelve under a leader. If you are a small group you will be called upon sometimes to play your part in one or more of these groups of twelve, but your spiritual group counterpart in the world of spirit consists also of twelve guiding spirits who will eventually call you, each one of you, to be their channels.

When you become a channel you submit your will completely to the will of God. The will of God is transmitted to you through your Third Guide. Your Third Guide will transmit his ray to you and, just as you are part of the earthly group of twelve, you will be part, during the hours of sleep, of that spiritual group of twelve. You will be sent out under the guidance of one of those radiant beings who belong in their several ways to one of the Seven Ashram within the Hierarchy.

The Hierarchy is preparing its descent to earth, and before the power can manifest through the Hierarchy great preparations must be made. There must be a certain number of channels ready to hold the power and those channels must be prepared to link soul and personality according to the Divine command.

With development comes that inner vision, the inner hearing of the Voice of God, that wonderful intuitive faculty which is like drops of golden light upon the ether.

You will not be called to do spectacular work. You must first of all prepare the way for the release of these vast Cosmic forces and you must be quite sure that the love of God is within your heart as light, so that those who come to use you as channels can find a resting place.

It is a long journey from the place of God to the earth, and at the end of that journey those who must fulfil this special work must find resting places where they can wait awhile before they are called upon to fulfil the next step on the path.

If we contemplate the Heavens we find innumerable stars, whose number cannot be named. We find great planets revolving in the ethers of space. All these planets, all these stars, all these signs and symbols, come under the guidance of the Hierarchy, and to them is transmitted identically the same ray as you are privileged to hold. Some are governed by one ray, some by another, but they link directly, via the Seven Types of Man and the Seven Root Races, with individual man through his chakra. That is the meaning of the science of Astrology.

Every word of yours, every thought, every sound you utter, every step you take, is caught upon every star and planet which is governed by your own particular ray, for the Seven Rays pass through your chakra. When your spiritual centres are unfolded there is one of those rays which is particularly your own and which links you with every minute star in the firmament of heaven. Therefore it is for you to make that star glow with the beauty of your own light or to become dark, and this is a great responsibility.